JOURNEY INTO
YOUR CENTER

JOURNEY INTO YOUR CENTER

Erhard Vogel, Ph.D.

Nataraja Publications

10171 Hawley Road

San Diego, California 92021

Nataraja Publications

10171 Hawley Road
San Diego, California 92021

ISBN 1-892484-05-6
Library of Congress Control Number: 00-132547

ATTENTION ORGANIZATIONS, HEALING & PAIN CENTERS, SCHOOLS OF SPIRITUAL DEVELOPMENT, YOGA & MEDITATION CENTERS: Quantity discounts are available on bulk purchases of this book for educational purposes, fund-raising or premium programs. Special books or book excerpts can also be created to fit specific needs. For information, please contact Nataraja Publications (619) 443-4164.

PHOTOGRAPHS BY ERHARD VOGEL

SECOND EDITION

This book is dedicated

to those who

share the light of reality

and contribute to

the cessation of suffering

thereby making a difference

with their life

and leaving a positive mark

on humanity.

OTHER PUBLICATIONS BY DR. ERHARD VOGEL

The Cave Meditation

This powerful meditation on CD comes to you from the direct experience of the world-renowned meditation master, Erhard Vogel, who dwelled in a Himalayan cave and teaches among the Himalayan sages. Allow yourself to be guided into a state of clear, focused consciousness in which all aspects of you rest in effortless balance in your center, reflecting the infinity of Being that you are. To hear a clip of this CD, please visit our website at **www.evogel.net**. $17.95

The Stress Release Response: 7 Steps To Triumph Over Stress

This CD contains a set of steps by which you can dependably free yourself from stress and its harmful effects—at a few moments' notice and at will. Dr. Vogel has taught tens of thousands of students from many parts of the world to effectively reduce stress. These students include members of such high-stress professions as hospice workers, doctors, lawyers, police officers, teachers and mothers. The Stress Release Response™ which he developed in the 1970s to answer an unmet need, has proven to be among the most beneficial means of coping with stress, yielding predictably positive results. To hear a clip of this CD, please visit **www.evogel.net**. $17.95

Centering Meditation

In this meditation you are guided in a unique and powerfully effective method of making the state of clear and centered consciousness directly available. Anyone who sincerely implements the step-by-step suggestions will create an inner state that is vibrant and attentive as well as deeply relaxed, thus overcoming internal struggles, mental distraction and the zoned-out state that is often mistaken for meditation. (Cassette tape) $9.95

Feelings And Emotions

Human experiences, including our feelings and emotions, are richly varied. However, we habitually repress our feelings because we fear they would overwhelm us. With this guided experience you will relate to your emotions with acceptance and become deeply in touch with your feelings. With repeated listening, you will open to ever more subtle levels and no longer experience your feelings as distractions but as enriching aspects of your self-experience. (Cassette tape) $9.95

The Healing Power Of Love

Imagine having everything about you in such a pure, clear and luminous state that your deepest insights and inner light shine forth in unrestricted strength. With this meditation, you will guide your faculties to harmonious union and thereby develop a powerful, peaceful love of yourself that creates healing from the physical to the deepest levels. (Cassette tape) $9.95

Yoga For Life

Erhard instructs you with clear, detailed description through a wide variety of yoga asanas in this two-tape set. Whether you are a beginner or advanced, you will find it easy to give yourself your own rejuvenating yoga classes at home. This will benefit you on all levels: developing flexibility and strength, deeply calming and centering the mind, creating a state of balance emotionally and on every level. You will use these tapes for years to come, growing healthier and more powerful in your concentration. (2 Cassette tapes) $46.50

Use the **Order Form** at the back of this book to purchase any of these publications **or visit our website at www.evogel.net**.

TABLE OF CONTENTS

In Gratitude. . .

I thank the luminous Himalayan sages Swamis Krishnananda and Chidananda for being such steady and devoted examples of life experienced in the joy of Being and for their loving friendship by which they have enriched my life; the Staff of the Nataraja Yoga Ashram for their devotion in managing the workings of the Ashram; Richard Bloeden for his generous and refined editing contributions; as well as my students for their sincere endeavors in making lasting positive change within themselves and humanity.

Dear Reader,

Most of us really want to succeed in life, even if we are afraid to or do not know how. We will not succeed without knowing the fundamentals to real and lasting success. Through the following chapters I hope to inspire and reinforce your expanding experience of the fundamentals by which you are able to direct your faculties knowingly toward your ultimate success and fulfillment.

Since the first printing of this book, I have learned about it from my students: doctors, lawyers, college students and housewives. These intelligent individuals read the same chapter daily for one week. An interesting thing occurs. At first reading they say to themselves, 'Hm, I understand that.' Next day, 'Oh, there is so much more.' Upon the third reading they discover even more. And so they continue to make the knowledge their own. A transformation takes place within. This book is not written to be scanned with the mind; it is to be read, experienced, realized.

I urge you to read with the focus and reflection that give you deep experience of yourself. This is a book for transformation, not mere accumulation of information. If, in the beginning, some of the concepts seem new or even foreign to you, trust in your ability to expand your perception with the experiences offered. As you continue in the book, you will experience the innermost You in increasing depth. Therein lies sheer delight.

ERHARD VOGEL

TO BEGIN WITH...

FLOURISHING IN
THE NEW MILLENNIUM

The new millennium is upon us. Within the psyche of humanity, deep internal stirrings have been taking place. This was verified for me when I heard my mother, before her eighty-second birthday, say to my sister, "The end of 1995 is coming up; that means we have only four years left until the year 2000—I can make that."

We reassess our lives at certain landmark events. At our birthdays, for example, we review our growth toward the fulfillment of our goals, we evaluate our level of well-being and refine our life plans. As a culture we ask ourselves every New Year how we have been doing and what we want to do about it. The change of millennia evokes a much larger, indeed a humanity-wide assessment. In this global evaluation we find voluminous evidence of humanity's profound accomplishments as well as abject failures.

To our dismay, an objective review of our history reveals centuries of war, carnage and mayhem, the enormous wastage of human energy and resources, the opposition to ourselves

3

and our potential. Through great technological advances we managed to make the twentieth century the bloodiest in human history. We now have the ability to cause our own extinction.

On the other hand, after the wars ended, did not even the victors share the sorrows of the vanquished and lead the efforts to rebuild what they had destroyed?

We have the capacity
to be creative rather than destructive,
to respond to reason rather than fear,
to treat each other with cooperation and love
rather than dissension and hatred.

In our assessment of the past millennium we can also see significant advancements that make it possible for us to enjoy a long life span of prosperity, health and freedom. The same advances in science, technology and communication that have increased our potential for destruction, have also made it possible for us to do profoundly more with our lives than merely struggle for daily survival. These advances have brought the nations and races of this earth into closer contact than ever before, empowering all humanity to prosper and grow with our shared wealth of resources and abilities.

Within humanity exist the wisdom, the caring and skill, as well as the resources required to transform the whole of humanity—all nations and cultures—into the highest enlightened and fulfilled state. This transformation will come to pass when we regard such an advanced state not merely as a theoretical ideal, or a fanciful flight of momentary notions, but as eminent practical reality. Leaving behind our history of conflict will make untapped powers available to all of humankind.

We are able to prevent our decline
only in the strength of our unity.

We can regard what is before us as skeptics and respond with doubt, or as victims—complain and blame. However, we can also choose to respond as empowered beings and face our future with trust and appreciation for the abilities and powers we own.

Thus we face a clear choice: will we allow ourselves to heedlessly run toward disaster in the new millennium, or will we regard our past as an enormous learning opportunity that inspires us to cultivate our constructive behaviors?

Assuming the constructive choice, we can now examine some of the significant life issues we are concerned with, and respond with positive behaviors as we have proven ourselves capable.

Let us assure that we flourish, not perish.

RELATING TO PRESENT CONCERNS

How can we relate to our present concerns from a realistic positive foundation? We could easily feel overwhelmed by the pervasiveness of our problems and forget the depth and power of our fundamental resources.

A university professor in Europe expressed to me his dismay over the state of the European political and cultural situation: the endangerment of culture, the polarization of society, the poisoning of the whole framework of life. While I am certainly able to empathize with his concern, I do not think the problem is unique to Europe.

Here in the United States, we also witness a rapidly accelerating deterioration of national as well as individual regard for values and principles, be they ethical, moral or aesthetic. It seems that anything deeper than experience on the most superficial, material level is frequently regarded with suspicion and responded to with hypocrisy. We suffer from a myopic viewpoint that has short-term material satisfaction as its focus. For example, we allow the extreme impracticality of despoiling the earth and its resources. While environmental concerns are expressed by some, they are considered an inconvenient expense by many.

We also notice in the United States an ever-widening rift between the over-privileged and the underprivileged. There is a persistent protest that most individuals are working in one way or another to contribute to the obscene wealth of the 5% who own 95% of the Gross National Product.

In the political arena, leaders of vision who could possibly guide the society into a direction that is more profound and meaningful, cannot get themselves elected. On the societal level, potential leaders are forced to compete with the public's addiction to mind-numbing empty commercial pablum that has become the opiate of the masses.

When we look at the challenges that present themselves to us, we may despair due to their sheer volume and variety. It helps to remember then, that the solution lies in us as individuals. As each one of us faces the future's challenges sincerely, expertly and persistently, we contribute to humanity's welfare and advancement. To begin the new millennium with a clean slate it behooves us to understand and remember:

Our problems
have their foundation
in the habitual distraction
from the experience and expression
of our true Self.
Our opportunities
have their foundation
in the conscious experience and expression
of the full strength and integrity
of the Being that we really are.

The Necessity Of Knowing Our Real Identity

It stands to reason that any organism living incongruous to itself will tend to perish. As human beings we have evolved to such a degree of strength and complexity that we are able to behave in ways which are incongruous to us, and yet survive. However, this survival is bought at extreme cost.

Being incongruous to ourselves seems to be the status quo in many of humanity's cultures. It means living in ways that are contrary to who we really are. Nevertheless, the question of our real identity is not frequently addressed.

We avoid facing ourselves, knowing who we are and thus claiming our life. We live a projected front that we hope is acceptable to society. There is a vague but persistent fear in us about exposing our real identity to the world, and even to ourselves. Therefore we end up fearing the simple and direct experience of our real identity and certainly the expression thereof as well. To cover this fear we seek distraction, involving our attention with objects and subjects other than our own Being.

Through distraction
we avoid facing ourselves.

At present our civilization is not so distracted by the demands of crisis imposed by world wars and their mass destruction. Could it be that we have found subtler ways of escaping the persistent internal demand to know ourselves, to be who we are, unhidden by the artificiality of self-created problems?

Understanding our tendency
toward self-evasion through distraction
sheds light on the anxiety, depression
and frantic pursuit of addictive involvements
so endemic in our time of "peace."

One would have to be nearly catatonic to not notice the increase of hecticness that characterizes life in our society—and the exponentially growing anger, neurosis and rigidity underlying both individual and public behaviors. These conditions are directly related to the sense of isolation that pervades our society.

Isolation is a function of egoism, for in egoism we regard ourselves as a separate body-mind complex. Egoism has become rampant.

> *It is important to recognize*
> *that egoism is not the result*
> *of society's unhealthy symptoms,*
> *but the cause.*

Egoism is based on a fundamentally erroneous concept regarding the absolute about ourselves: our identity. Ego is not our identity. It is a conception of ourselves as a severely limited physical-mental phenomenon—momentary, not absolute. Subjected to the delusions of the ego, we regard ourselves as isolated fragments, separate from the whole. We suffer from thinking of ourselves as basically flawed and lacking, therefore weak and at the mercy of innumerable threats beyond our control.

Such ways of thinking about ourselves do not relate to who we really are. Our real identity is one of infinitely greater potential. As soon as our mind, emotions, feelings—all our faculties—begin to relate to us in terms of who we really are, we notice a lessening of the problems. We experience an increase in our potential to lead our lives creatively, effectively and to our highest satisfaction.

Clearly, to take advantage of the opportunity offered to us by the new millennium, it is of principal importance for us to know our real identity—so important that we cannot afford to relate to it in terms of mere philosophical speculation. The impact of the mistaken ways in which we regard ourselves is painfully pervasive on all levels of life. Therefore it behooves us to consider our real identity with a deep sense of practicality.

We need to be absolutely certain about who and what we really are so that our faculties can realistically relate to us. They have to address us in clear consciousness, deeper in touch with nitty-gritty reality than our attachment to superficiality and falsity has allowed.

The direct relationship
between real Self and our faculties
needs to be permanently established;
every moment and event of daily life,
whether profound or mundane,
is to be related by each faculty
to our real identity.
Otherwise we miss out on our life.

It requires a sincere determination to make such a profound life-change. The reward is that we impart our experiences and expressions unto the Being we really are, and thereby cultivate a life of fulfillment.

BEING AN EXPERT IN LIFE

Contemporary life with its plethora of choices has become extremely challenging. We are busily engaged with so many activities absorbing our attention and energy that it seems we have nothing left for experiencing what is most important to us.

We must become expert not only at doing,
but also at being.

To be expert at being, we have to learn to value ourselves and our lives more than the objects and conditions to which we so often sacrifice our lives; we must learn to be expert in our life. We direct life according to what is important to the Being we really are. Our choices will then be fulfilling and successful in the real and lasting sense. Thus, we will not be mere victims of the haphazard, of circumstances and conditions, either on a personal, societal or humanity-wide level.

Within our society we have received years of education to prepare us for success in our jobs. Yet how much focused training have we received to become expert at leading our life with purpose and direction toward the fulfillment of our personal potential? Very little, by all accounts. Nonetheless, there is great expectation that somehow we should know what to do to be successful in all areas of life. We would actually benefit by becoming expert at such important life issues as conducting successful relationships—half our marriages now end in divorce—or becoming expert at being parents, and even more, at being ourselves. It is vitally important that we have knowledge of the fundamentals. This allows us to gain expertise in the important life issues. As we contemplate the new millennium we want to make sure we have the real knowledge.

To know what to do,
we need to know who we are.
To know who we are,
reveals what we really want.

With the attitude of becoming expert in life we can explore how to direct our choices toward the fulfillment of our real identity. We can sincerely delve into the heart of this fundamental topic and carefully examine what fulfills us lastingly as individuals and as humanity. The result will be profoundly more beneficial than our customary practice of devoting our energies to that which merely feels good for the moment, only to leave us feeling empty, disappointed and wanting more.

We can also grow into the practice of not merely talking about our important life issues, but devising specific strategies and practical steps by which we can predictably create powerful positive results.

For example, the issue of stress, while much talked about in our society, keeps growing out of control. We can learn powerful step-by-step methods by which—in less than one minute—we can predictably move from a state of tension and anxiety into a relaxed and secure state in which our faculties are firmly related to the power of our real Being. The dependable result is confidence and calmness. With these techniques we can easily seize control over the whole syndrome of stress, which has a stranglehold on the lives of many.

Our relationship to the environment is another pressing issue that needs to be resolved if we are to flourish during the new millennium. Consider the state of the earth.

One of the most powerful and pervasive influences upon our earth and its environment is the human being. Although we have proven through art and technology our capacity to contribute beauty and effectiveness, all too frequently our influence has, unfortunately, been negative.

Experts around the globe agree that we have already caused considerable damage to our planet. We have treated it with destructive disregard as if this earth were a worthless, disposable object instead of the home upon which humanity was born and nurtured.

Most animals know not to befoul their nest.
We human beings
befoul and poison our home
and treat it lowly.

If the internal state of human beings is toxic, unhealthy and in disarray, we will project this negative state upon our environment. If, however, the internal state of human beings is of integrity, clarity and health, we will create an environment that reflects and sustains our inner harmony.

Is it within humanity's potential to achieve such a positive state? Something deep within our core answers with a resounding 'Yes!'

FLOURISHING IN OUR REAL IDENTITY

We realize the ultimate positivity when we relate everything about us to the purity and wholeness that is our fundamental essence. As we focus our forces upon our essential Self, free of ego, we exert a powerful positive influence throughout our community and cause this positivity to grow throughout humanity. With sincere determination and actions performed with expertise, we can heal not only ourselves, but the entire earth.

Together let us determine to achieve this empowered state by learning to become expert at being true to who we really are, to our essential Self, our real identity. Let us learn through our own experience that the Being that we are is not some weak isolated ego, anxiously adrift in a hostile universe, competing for survival against all odds. May we experience that in reality we are interconnected Being; that is our real identity.

When we envision ourselves upon this tiny planet hurtling through interstellar space, we can gain the perception of ourselves as intimately interconnected with all forms of Being. As human beings we have evolved to a degree of consciousness that empowers us to realize our potential: to live and act in the awareness of our interconnectedness and thus be leaders on this globe in creating, nurturing and maintaining a powerfully healthy, harmonious and supportive life environment that is truly balanced and beneficial to all.

May we learn to realistically live as the interconnected Being that we are, and thereby be true to ourselves.

May we learn through direct experience to have our faculties—our mind and feelings, our intellect and intuition, even our body and senses—relate to us in terms of who we really are, and thereby be true to ourselves.

May we learn through proper training and practice to fine-tune, strengthen and direct these faculties so skillfully and effectively that we are able to conduct our lives with effortless balance toward lasting success in fulfillment, and thereby be true to ourselves.

May we realize our potential to relate to ourselves and to all with harmony and beneficence, living and acting with generosity born of the realization of our infinite wealth in interconnectedness.

For all of us to flourish in the new millennium, it is of fundamental importance for each one of us to create a powerful and lasting positive state within ourselves; through this we exert a beneficial influence all about ourselves.

Let us think globally, act locally,
and begin within.

BEING FULFILLED
IN WHO YOU ARE

CHAPTER ONE

FULFILLMENT
THE GOAL OF EVERY LIFE

A healthy life is one in which all aspects of your Being are functioning vitally and harmoniously, integrated in service of your chosen purpose. What is the purpose of your actions? Fulfillment. Ultimately, whatever you do has fulfillment as its purpose.

While all of us strive for it, fulfillment seems so rare and fleeting that some would even insist it is an illusion. Yet we know there are people whose lives are much closer to fulfillment than are others'.

> *It is not enough*
> *for us to be born,*
> *grow,*
> *reproduce,*
> *get fat and die.*

As human beings
we have enormous potential,
and it is our innate need
to fulfill that promise.
Indeed every one of our instincts,
yearnings, desires, ambitions and aspirations
has that as its real goal.

When you direct your life toward the fulfillment of your potential, you inevitably experience a sense of purpose, an inner harmony and accomplishment.

But often we misdirect the energy that tries to lead us toward real fulfillment. We settle for lesser objects of desire and, just as inevitably, experience a sense of futility, conflict and failure—the opposite of what we really want. We have short-changed ourselves and suffer in consequence.

It is like the person who has been invited to the grand gourmet feast of his life: he anticipates, prepares and hungers for the great event, but on his way to the feast he passes one of those many-flavor ice cream shops and in his hunger succumbs to the temptation to gorge himself on a banana split. When he arrives for the great feast, he is too stuffed and sick to take part in what he really wants.

Our urges and impulses can guide us or mislead us. The healthy and mature individual consciously decides which direction to take.

A life that is consciously and consistently
directed toward your goal,
the fulfillment of your total potential,
is a life of purpose
lived with vigorous enthusiasm,
with trust in yourself
and the universe you are part of.

That is a life of real health and success, for it is free of the chronic self-limitations and frustrations from which many suffer. Those negative factors eat away at us like insidious cancers.

Who wants to be healthy in life? With the exception of aberrations, we could safely say everybody. However, we seldom understand what real health is. In our society we often fail to consider that the healthy state includes not just the body, but also the mind, emotions and feelings, even the intuitive faculty. The healthy state integrates everything about you with your real meaning.

Can a way of life be healthy or fulfilling when it is contradictory to the meaning of your Being? Of course it cannot.

Anything that is contradictory
to the meaning of your Being
will frustrate you,
expending your life energy in confusion,
rationalization and self-opposition.
It will have you feeling angry,
empty, lacking and yearning.

However, it is a common problem that as soon as we consider the meaning of our Being, we tend to relegate it to the field of philosophy and treat this most fundamental topic as if it belonged to the realm of the highfalutin theoretical. Instead of welcoming a clear understanding of our life's foundation, we tend to seek refuge behind fancy talk that we may pull out of a special drawer on Sunday mornings or at cocktail parties.

When we speak realistically of the meaning of our Being, we are not interested in discussing some distant theoretical concept. We would not gain much benefit from that. You do benefit profoundly, though, when you relate to the meaning of your Being as the nitty-gritty practicality of your life.

The fundamental meaning of who and why you are deserves to be related to in a manner that is at once rational and all-inclusive, not limited to a myopic point of view. If you are not true to the meaning of your Being, what good is anything else?

CHAPTER TWO

BEING AN EXPERT AT FULFILLMENT

One of the most important factors we all share is the innate need for real fulfillment. Not one of us is exempt from that, whether you are old or young, male or female, rich or poor. Everything you do and think and feel is ultimately directed toward fulfillment. Although each one of us may define fulfillment in our own way, we all have the potential to reach fulfillment.

To dedicate yourself
consciously, consistently and intelligently
to real fulfillment
clearly is the advantageous course of action
for you to take in life.

Although comprehending the advantage of dedicating yourself to fulfillment is a necessary step toward making your life fulfilling, it is not enough. To act upon this comprehension is the logical next step.

Many have attempted throughout their lives to fulfill their potential, and yet failed. This does not prove, as is so often assumed, that it cannot be done; the right approach is absolutely necessary.

You might aspire to being a successful brain surgeon and having the benefits which go along with that profession. Yet you would not think of performing brain surgery merely on the merit of your aspiration. You know that you would have to study and practice long and hard to become expert in the field of surgery before ever reaping the benefits.

When we aspire to fulfillment,
why do we act as if the mere aspiration
were enough?

Fulfillment, being so much higher a reward than being a successful brain surgeon, teacher, architect, lawyer, business person or whatever profession we may choose, obviously deserves more of our application, and certainly not less. Yet, when in a moment of inspiration we make a faint stab at fulfillment and do not immediately succeed, we become disappointed and quit.

The fulfillment of your potential
is the greatest achievement in life.
Therefore it calls for
the utmost
of your attentiveness and expertise.

Though many of us may be expert in our occupation, few of us have recognized the obvious benefit of being expert at our own life. However, the greatest pleasure lies in the act of fulfilling ourselves. To direct our life consciously to real fulfillment is its own reward.

Most goals yield their reward
only when achieved,
but from the moment you sincerely
dedicate yourself and your actions
to a life true to its meaning,
you experience direct benefits.

The rewards include, but are not limited to, a deep sense of ease, increasing self-respect and confidence, greater success at work and in your relationships, and a steadily growing feeling of absolute self-acceptance that yields inner tranquillity and joyous satisfaction.

What if there were a systematic approach by which you could be guided step-by-step through such clear experiences that you would gain a deep understanding of who you really are and what you really need in order to be fulfilled? There is no sense in investing any energy in trying to fulfill yourself when you do not even know what does fulfill you.

Ask yourself, 'What fulfills me individually? Not what I think society wants me to say, but what do I come up with when no one is watching and I do not have to have any fancy ideas? What do I really need to be fulfilled when I consider myself not like an adolescent dependent, but as a responsible adult?'

You know this is your life. You can enthusiastically face its challenges as opportunities to make life really successful. What if there were a systematic approach by which you could strengthen and fine-tune yourself to achieve that ultimate life success, that lasting fulfillment?

Well, there is!

CHAPTER THREE

FULFILLMENT THROUGH BECOMING AN EXPERT IN LIFE

Once you have recognized that fulfillment does not just happen but requires a systematic approach, the next practical consideration is, 'With the faculties that I have, what can I realistically expect to attain in terms of fulfillment in this, my actual life?' This is quite naturally followed by the question, 'What must I do now to attain fulfillment?'

You would certainly make a careful analysis of the fundamentals if you wanted to succeed in business. Do not your success and fulfillment in life deserve at least this much care?

You may also ask yourself, 'Am I willing to do what needs to be done for fulfillment?' If not, what is the sense in doing anything else?

There is actually no choice: the innermost urge for fulfillment is always there, demanding to be answered. You could, however, treat these questions as such an enormous challenge that you stumble for years in confused efforts. It need not be so.

You can utilize a proven step-by-step approach to realistically address the vitally important questions regarding your fulfillment and their answers. Is there such a comprehensive, realistic approach? Yes, the Expert In Life™ approach.

There are specific ways
in which you can gain the expertise
that empowers you
to bring yourself closer and closer
to the fulfillment of your potential,
ways that,
when properly and consistently employed,
make you a healthier
stronger clearer brighter being.

Just think, with such ways available, is it not most practical and advantageous for you to become expert in those ways, and institute them in your life directly?

Here are specific tools now, by which you develop your life expertise. You practice observing your behaviors objectively so you can clearly see which are beneficial and which are harmful to you. To recognize in detail your negative tendencies and positive alternatives is of enormous benefit. You will be amazed how the ensuing awareness increases your constructive choices.

You learn to align yourself subtly and powerfully with behaviors through which you steadily experience and creatively express the strength and full capacity of your real Being. Thus involved in positivity, you free your energies from all actions, feelings and thoughts contrary to your well-being.

You practice specific ways of cultivating a vital and fulfilling life physically, sensually and psychologically, as well as mentally, intellectually and intuitionally. This allows your subtler instruments of awareness to come to the fore and bring you in touch with the most underlying, fundamental aspect—your essence, the Being that you really are. Such a focus gives meaning to the way you conduct your life.

With deep self-knowledge it is easier for you to properly care for yourself. You live a significantly healthier life, and at the same time accomplish so much more; you thrive with your work, and your relationships flourish; you stop the addictive behaviors by which so many limit themselves.

> *The process of becoming expert*
> *at leading your life*
> *gives you a greater*
> *understanding of yourself.*
> *As a result,*
> *you experience a deep sense*
> *of self-appreciation.*
> *This gives you the motivation*
> *to free yourself from self-destructive habits:*
> *they feel too repulsive.*

To liberate your faculties from the habits and tendencies to which they have been subjected since your early years, you must transform them and their behaviors. You achieve this by persistently establishing your faculties in a loyal relationship with who you are and thereby releasing them from their enmeshment with the empty false self.

Through a well-rounded, thoroughly tested strategy of becoming expert at your life, you learn to transform your faculties. For example, you fine-tune the body step-by-step into a healthy and vibrant instrument—one that is responsive to your requirements in an attitude of effortlessly balanced poise. You practice specific powerful breathing techniques by which you can significantly increase your energy level and strengthen your physical balance and mental clarity, while noticeably empowering your intellectual and intuitional faculties.

In this multifaceted approach of seizing life expertise, you learn through your own experience to understand the mind in intimate detail. You cultivate the ideal state of mind and free yourself from tendencies that oppose this state. You learn the causes and costs of distraction, and how to actively overcome them. You train your mind to be in a state of steady concentration at will and to become a powerful and subtle instrument of fulfillment.

The list goes on. The Expert In Life approach is filled with specific and powerful means by which you can deeply and positively transform your faculties and behaviors to consciously live according to your life meaning and purpose, steadily and clearly progressing toward the fulfillment of your potential. Great joy and endless possibility open up to you when you set out with the proper means—with sincerity and enthusiasm, with continuity and trust in yourself—to become an Expert In Life.

CHAPTER FOUR

UNDERSTANDING
THE PURPOSE OF YOUR LIFE

In this age of materialism it has become fashionable to maintain that there is no purpose to life. In a misinterpretation of existentialism you may exclaim, "Live and be merry today, for tomorrow you may die and that'll be the end of that."

Even Sartre may not have meant his existential declarations to be followed as seriously as many have. How do we know that he was not some Gauloise-smoking young man on the Left Bank who wanted to impress the girls and evoke their maternal instincts with an attitude of sadness bordering on nihilism? Could his statements regarding human existence have had the simpler motive of inducing them to pull his sad head to their nurturing bosom? How do we know?

Much of our culture has skidded into a lazy disregard of life's meaning and purpose due to sensual avarice, emotional emptiness and intellectual bankruptcy.

In fact, if you were to ask your own friends, "What is the purpose of your life?"—what kind of response would you receive? Quite likely they would look at you with concern and ask if you were all right. Ask yourself, 'What is the reason for my life?' Are you able to come up with a clear answer?

This question and its answer are not a philosophical luxury, but a practical necessity.

> *How can you expect yourself*
> *to successfully lead your life,*
> *if you do not know its purpose?*

Recently I attended the opening of a large urban shopping center. There was one shop that attracted more attention than the others—a gadget shop. People spent a long time in there figuring out the purposes of the gadgets. They were fascinated.

Place an appliance that people have not seen before into your home sometime. Notice their reaction: "What is its purpose? How does it work?"

When you ask about the purpose of a thing, you are asking, "How is it fulfilling its function?" When you ask, "What is this thing's function or purpose?"—you are asking about the reality of it. The German word for reality is "Wirklichkeit," that which ultimately works. This exemplifies the relationship between function and reality. In regard to yourself, most of all, you need to know—and often we do not—what the purpose of your life is, what the reality of your Being is.

> *Only by knowing the reality of your Being*
> *can you make your life work*
> *and fulfill its purpose.*
> *Only then can you find*
> *the fulfillment you seek.*

To say there is no purpose to life is a practical absurdity. Imagine if there were really no purpose to your life—you would not get out of bed in the morning; there would be no reason to.

Without reason there is no pleasure. Without reason and pleasure there is no motivating force in our life. We then feel despondent and lethargic, experiencing life as boring and depressing, not as the great gift that life is.

Fortunately, life is not without purpose. Everything in nature has its purpose. Why should that exclude our life?

There is a definite purpose to your life.

> *Your life is there to be experienced.*
> *That is your life's purpose:*
> *to experience **that** you are,*
> *and **what** you are,*
> ***as** you are.*

To fulfill that purpose means to live your life from moment to moment in conscious acknowledgement of the power and the beauty, the miracle of Being that in reality you are. That is the ultimate fulfillment, the lasting pleasure for which your life strives.

CHAPTER FIVE

LIVING SINCERELY
ACCORDING TO YOUR IDEAL

Every March—like clockwork—the swallows return to Capistrano; you can depend on it. They have traveled for many miles, endured great hardships and, I am sure, have come across many a temptation to do something else.

They do not dally because it is still nice and warm where they happen to be, or because obstacles present themselves; nor will the discovery of a new field filled with succulent insects dissuade them from their appointed rounds. They have a mission to fulfill, and the meaning of their lives lies in the fulfillment of that mission: to build their nests, lay their eggs, hatch and rear their young in San Juan Capistrano. They will subjugate every other desire to that mission; every action only has relevance in relation to it. Their lives are busily—and seemingly happily—dedicated to that purpose.

Your life, too, has a purpose. As you are of a higher degree of evolution, your purpose is correspondingly more complex than the mere response to the instincts for survival and reproduction.

You have the potential to respond
to all the impulses of existence
on all levels,
to experience in full consciousness
the wholeness of Being.

That is your mission. That is the reason for your being.

You, too, fare best when you do not succumb to the temptation of distractions, when you subjugate your passing desires to the way of life that is dedicated to your real purpose, and when you recognize that every action only has relevance in relation to it.

Then you live according to that which has lasting value, independent of time and circumstance. It will not be the highest priority one day and be superseded on another. Nor will there be something else that will give you greater fulfillment. It is your ideal.

We call one who lives in constant relationship to the ideal an "idealist." In our society we regard an idealist with derision, as a dreamer, out of touch with reality. But quite the contrary is true.

As an idealist you clearly set your sights
on the ultimate aim;
you live and act in accord with that,
giving direction and meaning to your life.
That is not being a dreamer or a fool;
it is only being intelligent.
The idealist is the practical realist.

If anyone is to be regarded as foolish, it must surely be the person who keeps dedicating his life to actions that repeatedly and predictably yield failure and disappointment.

Living sincerely according to an ideal
takes a person out of the limited ego concept;

it elevates the ordinary person
to a great person.

Albert Einstein was such a one. He observed early in his life that most people expend the majority of their life energy on momentary desires and petty problems. When he was about thirteen or fourteen years old, he decided he was not going to dissipate his life in such silly involvements. Einstein lived true to that decision, and you need only look at his pictures to see the deep fulfillment radiating from his face. Madam Marie Curie, the great physicist, also comes to mind when we think of real idealists, as do Dr. Albert Schweitzer, Dr. Martin Luther King, Mahatma Gandhi and Abraham Lincoln. They did not merely think and talk about their ideals, they lived them.

There is no actual way
to succeed with your actions
unless you relate them
to that which ultimately and lastingly
fulfills you.

At times you may be deceived by the appearance of success, when you have directed your actions toward some transient goal. But when you do not integrate your actions with the meaning of your Being, failure, disappointment and frustration are sure to follow.

It is up to you to choose the type of action to which you dedicate your life moments. In one way or another, active or passive, you always make a choice. That is your privileged opportunity as well as your inevitable responsibility. You might as well make your choice consciously and wisely by the application of your intelligent free will.

CHAPTER SIX

A HEALTHY LIFE REQUIRES KNOWING YOUR REAL IDENTITY

What if, by some quirk of mind, you were to identify yourself as something you are not, say a frog? You could, with all ambition and skill, work hard and steadily to acquire everything for which a frog dreams. You could have abundant food and all the delicacies a frog fancies, a wonderful home (for a frog) and the most beautiful frog or frogess in frogdom as your mate. Now, even if you were utterly convinced that you were a frog, would you, a human being, be really fulfilled living on insects in a slimy pond married to a frog?

The underlying reality of the Being that you are will not be permanently denied. It is always there and will assert itself until it is related to by your faculties, your instruments of self-experience and expression.

There is one factor without which you can be neither successful nor fulfilled: the knowledge of your real identity. Why is that knowledge so crucial?

You are almost continuously engaged in action. The ultimate purpose of all your actions is to bring you closer to fulfillment.

> *It stands to reason*
> *that if you address your actions,*
> *indeed your whole life,*
> *to some mistaken idea of who you are*
> *and not to the Being that you really are,*
> *you will ultimately feel disappointed,*
> *frustrated and empty,*
> *no matter how hard you work.*

Why would we address our lives to some mistaken idea of who we are? Because many of us simply do not know our real identity. It is a well-known fact that psychologists and psychiatrists are kept busy because of innumerable people in our society suffering from identity crisis.

Ask yourself for a moment, 'Who am I really? What am I?' These are not idle questions; the answer to these questions is the practical and necessary foundation for the meaningful and fulfilling life we all want.

What was your answer? Usually we answer, 'I am a woman,' or 'I am a man,' or 'I am a plumber, lawyer, housewife,' or 'I am Jane Doe.'

But we are beings, not bodies and genders, not functions and labels: they only augment our Being. To identify ourselves in terms of our bodies, functions or labels constitutes a false identification and is as detrimental and dissatisfying as identifying ourselves as frogs.

Nor does it benefit us to confuse our identity with our mind, as we are prone to do.

Just as you do not mistake
the mirror reflecting your image
for your identity,
so must you not mistake
your mind reflecting you
for your real Self.

Now let us consider the mind.

Mind is not your identity;
it is but an instrument
through which your real identity
is to be experienced.

It is necessary for you to remain aware of this fundamental fact, if you are to employ your mind properly in the service of a meaningful and satisfying life.

We will investigate the nature of our real identity more as we continue. For now, consider some fundamental factors of real identity:

Your real identity
is the irreducible something about you,
the essence that you permanently are,
independent of time,
circumstance and condition,
that without which you could not be;
it is your very Beingness.

When all is said and done, when all modifications have been stripped away, the irreducible something about you remains: the fact that you are.

> *What you are is **that** you are.*
> *As the ancients said,*
> *"I am that, that I am."*

To relate to yourself as a mind would be a mistake. Your mind changes frequently as it is easily affected by the vicissitudes of circumstances and conditions.

Here is a simple test: observe your mind for a few moments, right now, in silence. Note how mind tends to jump from one thing to another. You can direct it though, to become calm.

Direct your mind toward calmness. Simply tell your mind, 'Be calm now.' Give it something to hold on to, like quietly becoming absorbed in watching your breathing. Let mind humbly flow with the rhythm of your breath.

Observe mind growing calmer and calmer. Enjoy, let yourself go into the experience. For just a few moments, observe your own mind in the calmer state.

Now, who was observing the mind? Who was directing mind to become calmer? That silent observer and director is the real you, the real identity that you are.

Only when you have established your mind in the correct relationship with your real identity can you expect mind to serve you. Usually it is the other way around; we seem forced to enslave ourselves in the service of mind.

In a fulfilled life, your mind is thinking of you as the Power of Being, the subtle energy by which you are. Along with mind, everything else—your feelings and emotions, intellect and intuition, even your senses and body—will then relate to you according to your real identity.

To establish all your faculties in the proper relationship with who you really are, is indispensable to your being Expert In Life,™ to sincerely seeking a way of life that is healthy, successful and fulfilled. You can do that.

CHAPTER SEVEN

THE SPIRIT THAT YOU ARE

To fulfill yourself, you must know yourself. To know what you really are, look not at what you are now and then, but what you are permanently, intrinsically and essentially.

Many things about you have changed since your infancy. Your body has grown, your mind matured. As an adult you feel, think and act differently than you did in childhood. Yet in essence you are still the Being that came into this world on the day of your birth. This essence is the permanent aspect about you. The permanent endures infinitely, independent of time and circumstance; it is transcendent.

There is a tendency to be so absorbed in the momentary emotions or events, that you feel as if they were your very Being; you identify yourself with them. However, they are merely momentary emotions or events. If you invest them with your identity, you lose touch with your real Being.

The emotions, sensations, feelings and events that may have seemed so critically important, pass on and are soon forgotten. Your identity remains; it is what you always are.

That which is permanent about you, your identity, is also intrinsic to you—being of your innermost nature and inseparable from it.

> *What is your innermost nature,*
> *that without which you could not be?*
> *We call that "essence."*
> *Your essence is*
> *the absolute,*
> *irreducible*
> *substance of you.*

The essence is that which upholds everything about you. It is your unchanging identity. The word "essence" is derived from the Latin root "esse," to be, from which our word "is" is derived. You are what you are in essence. Your essence is the power by which you are, the Power of Being; your essence is that you are.

> *The essential Power of Being*
> *is the permanent aspect,*
> *the real identity that you always are,*
> *to which you need to relate your life*
> *in order to enjoy real satisfaction.*

However, this essence, this most important and fundamental Beingness of you, is often neglected or even regarded as unreal merely because it cannot be perceived by the senses. Most of us are accustomed to regard what we can see or touch as real, and anything we cannot see or touch as unreal. Actually, it is the other way around.

It is generally agreed that the senses can only perceive phenomena and events, the passing. The passing phenomena and events are only momentary appearances, like the images on a movie screen, which you certainly would not consider substantial or real. Remember, physics describes objects as momentary phenomena caused by the coming and going of atoms. Thus, what your senses alone perceive is not real. Only you as knowing Being are capable of perceiving the full reality.

There cannot be only ephemeral events; there has to be something underlying—some substance out of which these events arise.

The word "substance," derived from Latin, denotes that which stands under, the underlying. It is your foundation and structure, what you fundamentally are.

In the human being, substance is not something of weight and shape; that is only temporary appearance again, not real. The reality of you, your substance, that which permanently and intrinsically stands under all aspects of you, is your essence, your Beingness.

Essence is also referred to as "spirit." In chemistry, spirit is the essence of something, the distillate, the refined, the pure substance you have left after extracting all dross.

Your real identity,
that which you fundamentally are,
is neither
a momentary conglomeration of particles
called body,
nor a neurological event
called mind,
but the essential subtle force
by which you are:
spirit.

I am usually loathe to employ this word, "spirit," for in our society it tends to conjure up fantasy images like syrup dripping from silver-lined clouds. I indulge myself carefully and sparingly in the use of this much-abused, but so important, term.

When we speak of the spirit of something, we speak of its true intent, its very meaning, as in the spirit of the law. Thus your spirit is the meaning, the true intent of your existence.

We relate spirit to loyalty and devotion, as when we speak of team spirit. Clearly, spirit is what is fundamentally most important to you and about you.

To live in loyalty and devotion to your spirit is called a spiritual life. It only makes sense to live according to your fundamental priority.

It is important
that you relate to your spiritual life
not as a fantasy
to be engaged in once a week,
or now and then,
not as a theoretical, philosophical
or religious luxury
to be indulged in
when it strikes your fancy,
but as fundamental and permanent reality.

Thus, to live realistically means to have your mind and feelings, indeed all your instruments of awareness, relate loyally to you in terms of your real identity, the spirit that you are.

Your spirit is your essential identity, that which you really are. That is what you need to know in order to know yourself, to fulfill yourself.

FINDING THE
PATH TO FULFILLMENT

CHAPTER EIGHT

SELF-MOTIVATION TOWARD SUCCESS

We each have our own idea of what we mean by a successful life. Though we may differ in our descriptions of it—one person's dream may be another's nightmare—all of us yearn and act to find real fulfillment: to arrive at that unique state in which we experience relationship with all, where nothing is wanting. A life dedicated to that goal may be considered a successful one.

WHAT DO YOU WANT?

To know what you want in life is obviously important. So ask yourself, 'What is it that I really want? Not what I think I ought to want, not what others may want, but what do I want?'

When I ask that question to large groups of people, the response usually is silence, followed by confusion.

Is it not strange that such a simple question can raise such consternation? What you want motivates everything you feel, think and do, yet most people cannot come up with a simple answer to the question. Consequently, they squander most of their time and energy—indeed, their lives—pursuing objects which, once gained, only disappoint them.

Those who pursue the ultimate aim, idealists, are the only practical realists, inasmuch as they let their actions be directed by their one source of fulfillment—by what they really want. Such lives have direction and meaning; such lives are ones of success.

The Voice Within

Now you may ask, 'How can I know, really, what I want?'

Have you not had experiences of knowing something without having heard or read it before? Somehow, you know. Or, perhaps while reading a particular idea, something within you knows it is true, though the idea may not have occurred consciously to you before. How do you know?

There resides in you
an Inner Knower,
a true reference point to knowledge.
When you silence the voices of fear,
prejudice and distortion,
you can hear the serene, honest voice
of inner wisdom
guiding you with its utterly reliable truth.

Thus, do not waste your time looking for the answer to that all-important question on the outside; all you usually find there are other people's interpretations, along with their self-evasions and rationalizations. Look honestly within and assume responsibility for what you find.

Have you found out what you really want, and are you acting accordingly? Ask yourself, 'Am I usually responding to a fleeting fancy, or is my life continuously propelled by something that has always been at the core of me?'

Remember this: It is the permanent
that relates you to reality.
It is the underlying aspiration
which has always been there
that reveals to you what you really want.

OBSTINATE OBSTACLES

We may all agree that a successful life—a life relating realistically to fulfillment—is our ultimate desire. But the fact is, not many people are leading such a life. What, then, are the obstacles to success?

The root cause
of all failure and suffering
is ignorance regarding our identity.

Ignorance is manifested in terms of false conception and illusion. Your whole life can be viewed as a drive to fulfill Self. If you are ignorant of that drive, or have a mistaken idea of what really fulfills you, or do not even know who that Self is, how can you fulfill yourself? Impossible. Ignorance is our fundamental obstacle.

Ignorance, false conception and illusion are but one great distraction preventing us from experiencing life as it is in reality. To seek refuge in such distraction seems unthinkable. Yet many in our society tenaciously cling to falsity and illusion, willingly squandering time and energy for their many diversions.

Because of ignorance, we suffer from a very limited idea of what we are. Consequently, our ideals are limited as well. Limited ideals mean limited goals. Limited goals are easily attained, but not satisfying. They leave us feeling full but not fulfilled, like the proverbial Chinese meal. We want something more and mistakenly assume that we want more of the same. This results in ever-deepening cycles of frustration. The thrust of our lives toward fulfillment is then diverted until we finally break out of the rut.

The longer you stay in a rut,
the deeper you dig yourself in
and the harder it is to climb out.

Let us say you look for a job in order to make enough money to pay your pressing bills. Unemployed, you anticipate how happy you would be if you just had a job. But soon after you have received a few pay checks, your eagerness to work subsides; you were motivated by need. Eliminate the need with a few pay checks, and you have eliminated the motivation as well. If the motivation were of a higher order than just making money, it would take more than money to satisfy it, and thus serve you longer.

Lack of motivation, another obstacle on the quest to real success, is a terrible blight, as anyone who has suffered boredom can attest to. If the management of our corporations would stimulate in their workers higher motivational forces—such as the joy of participation, creative contribution, responsibility-sharing and ultimately, self-expression—they could reverse the steady decline in productivity and quality that plagues our industry.

Ignorance gives us false ideas
of who we are
and, consequently,
creates ever-growing cycles of false desires
that lead to mounting frustration.

Ignorance also gives rise to fear: we are fearful when we are not in touch with our real Being. Without the touchstone of knowing ourselves, we lack the basis of contact with everything else.

Fear keeps many of us attached to self-limiting cycles. Even when we know we are so deep in a rut that the earth seems to be closing in on us, choking off our light and air, we sometimes fight for our right to dig in even deeper. Our conditioning—those patterns of reaction and behavior ingrown over so many years—seems to rule our lives whether we like it or not, whether it is good for us or not.

Then we easily fall into the trap of rationalizing: 'I should not really expect much of my life. After all, I am only human.'

Only human? As human beings we possess wonderful faculties and great skills that have brought us to a high evolutionary level. Who or what else should express the grandeur of the universal process, if not the human being?

Yes, it is difficult to break old patterns, especially since they seem to afford the comfort of familiarity, no matter how miserable they make us feel. How comforting though, is the familiarity of misery?

We may also suffer from such obstacles as inertia, laziness and procrastination. We may seek refuge in our weaknesses, but the fact is that we cannot halt the process of our evolution. Eventually, our problems will take on crisis proportions, forcing us out of our false complacency.

FACING AND TRANSCENDING OBSTACLES

There is a force within you
that will never be denied:
the urge for total expression of Self.

Any attempt to suppress an aspect of yourself will only result in that aspect asserting itself with redoubled force until it breaks free. Any attempt to limit, or in other ways distort or distract the drive of self-expression will eventually be thwarted by that relentless inner will, which is far deeper and subtler than your other processes. This is nothing but reality exerting itself.

You are an integral aspect of the limitless universe; anything that obscures this truth will have to suffer in a clash with reality. Every experience you undergo tends to contribute to the revelation of truth. If you resist, the point has to be more forcefully, if not violently made.

Resistance to reality
is the cause of suffering;
acceptance of reality
is the seed of success.

It is in its inalterability that your innate drive toward self-expression reveals its relationship to your ultimate desire: the two are one. Your most constant and all-pervasive desire is to express yourself totally and in reality. And here is revealed the enormous power of your real desire.

Nothing,
be it ignorance or forgetfulness,
illusion or laziness,
or anything else,
can stand in the way
of the relentless flow
toward total expression and realization
of all the aspects of the Power of Being.

So let us stop torturing ourselves with doubt and fear and falsity. Let us no longer discourage ourselves from experiencing what we really want by continuously conjuring up innumerable ways by which we cannot have it. Instead, let us align our forces and channel our energy so we will experience, indeed, that we can!

CHAPTER NINE

THE FEAR OF SUCCESS

The person whose life is characterized by failure is usually not incapable of success, but afraid of it. This is a fact not easily admitted to by one who, for all appearances' sake, works so hard to succeed. But have not most of us observed relatives, friends or acquaintances who seem to experience life as a succession of failures?

A man—let us call him Fred for convenience—came to me for spiritual counseling after he had suffered a series of setbacks that included a car accident, a bout with severe illness, separation from his wife and a long list of minor mishaps. He had risen to considerable social standing after graduating from a prestigious medical school and working as a surgeon in an important hospital. But he considered himself a failure.

When I asked Fred whether he ever got the feeling that life was trying to tell him something, he replied, "More accurately, I think it's out to get me!"

Fred's feeling
that a force outside himself
was responsible
for the direction and quality of his life
is characteristic of someone
locked into a failure pattern.

As Fred talked more about himself, it became clear that this attitude of dependency was firmly entrenched in his life. In fact, though he had risen to a position of great responsibilities, Fred had never assumed full responsibility for the course of his life.

This situation is much more prevalent than we may wish to acknowledge. It is firmly rooted in our earliest experiences.

We all grow up taking our cues from parents and elders. As an infant, your life consists largely of a response pattern to parental directives. You learn to survive in this vast, unknown world by subtly sensing your primary caretakers' approval and disapproval, their smiles and frowns, cooing and scolding, the offering or withdrawal of the sustenance and love you need. By judging your caretakers' responses, you decide how to act and even how to feel.

In adolescence, though, you are told, "You're on your own now. Make your own decisions; determine your own responses. Claim this life and lead it as yourself now, as the Being you are." That is when the dreaded struggle of adolescence arises. The call to become free from dependency demands to be answered. All too often though, this urge for inner maturity is reduced to silence by the insistent demands of habits urging you to remain bound to the imagined safety of the familiar.

It seems extremely difficult to break the patterns so familiar since those days of infancy and childhood. The hazily remembered security of the past seems threatened by change.

The sheer force of the call within
may even be interpreted
as alien and frightening.
Yet it persists.
Your Being
wants to be experienced and expressed
wholly and freely,
as it is.

The drive toward freedom and self-sufficiency has always been there, but arises at special moments from the innermost recesses of our Being with tremendous strength. Until this drive is responded to, we suffer from a dilemma between dedicating our life to the expectations of others and claiming our life for the experience and expression of our Being.

Our friend, Fred, handled the dilemma by becoming extremely busy, not with resolving the conflict, but with an ambitious new college career. He felt this was a project so demanding of his awareness that he had no energy left to heed the inner call to live his own life.

Of course, he was not going to admit to himself that he had sold out, that he had squelched his own creative force, his very Being which had wanted to rise to full expression.

So it goes with any of us who refuse to bear the responsibility for our Being. Individuals who have given up this responsibility usually do not admit that they have relinquished their individuality—and the accompanying privileges and responsibilities—because of fear. They are not that responsible; that is the nature of their problem. They will try to place the responsibility for their decisions, their feelings and fears, indeed their entire life on something else, be it circumstances, conditions or other people.

The greater the self-deception,
the more intricate the veil of rationalizations
woven to obscure the truth.

Growth consists of a graduation from dependency to independence. For this you need to nurture a fundamental condition of respect and even kindness toward yourself. Then you can give to yourself the thrill of being the director of your life, truly and clearly responsive to your challenges. Failures and successes can be related to with a sense of independence, all integrated as experiences of Being.

CHAPTER TEN

DARE TO BE

The Power of Being by which each one of us is, must be allowed to see the light of day, to be recognized, to be lived by us. Nothing can forever suppress it.

As long as we deny the truth of our Being,
we force it to exert itself
with redoubled power
until it eventually explodes
within or upon us.
Usually this takes the form of crisis.

Remember Fred? He ran into failure and crisis by trying to evade the challenge of claiming responsibility for himself. He kept himself busy and distracted with what otherwise could have been integral parts of a rewarding life. First came schooling and internship, then the demanding problems of launching a career. By marrying and raising a family he ensured that his attention would continue to be totally occupied by outer demands.

His wife, Myrna, also avoided facing herself. She had left the safety of her family and answered her crisis of self-determination by attaching her life to a series of "boy-friends," until she found Mr. Right, Fred, who she had hoped would continue where her parents had left off. It had seemed to be a rather snug solution: Fred, the provider, taking care of battling the outside world, while Myrna bore children and cared for the home. Fred lived what Myrna had been afraid to face, while Myrna expressed what Fred had so carefully avoided in his life.

They called this love. They never bothered to ask whether one person should or even could live to express what another has suppressed.

Their activities, in themselves, could have provided admirable means to the expression of life. But Fred and Myrna used them as distractions to evade the reality of their lives.

Reality is not to be denied though. All the evasive maneuvers were eventually exhausted: the backbreaking pace of school had ended; the romance of falling in love had given way to the disappointments of unfulfilled fantasies; the children were almost grown up.

There was time now: time to think, time to once again become aware of the inner stirrings. The happiness he had been so busily running after remained elusive. Fred felt frustrated, empty, still a failure.

By now he had learned to fear those moments when feelings buried deeply within tried to arise. He feared his feelings; he feared facing himself; he sought refuge in things alien: he failed.

Fred finally noticed that the more he struggled to achieve happiness by amassing outside objects, the more his life disintegrated. He failed at work. His relationship with his wife reached such a point of stress that there was hardly any love left to lose between them. As a father, he did not do much better.

Myrna and Fred thought they would look for help among the "alternate lifestyles." They had not been able to open themselves to a marriage counselor, so they tried a bit of this and a bit of that "self-help" program. Fred and Myrna shopped for holy masters, even trying a famous miracle-worker for a while. They picked and selected like spiritual fast-food addicts, gulping the superficial and spitting out the essential. They remained dissatisfied.

It was not until life had dealt him serious accidents and crises that Fred finally felt forced to make some real changes. But even then, the tendency to escape when something started to work, kept arising. The old habits of self-destruction proved hard to overcome, but continuing with those habits made life even harder.

Fred is not alone in his self-evasion. His behaviors are but a composite of common failure patterns. There are those who constantly construct failures to distract themselves. They say they are pursuing truth while they are actually running after illusion. They program themselves for failure.

People can concentrate so much of their effort
on lamenting life's failures
that they have no moments left
to enjoy life's successes.

In the habit of focusing on failure, they then feel compelled to prove that they were right all along with their negative expectations. When they find something by which they could be effective, they apply it in such a manner that it has to fail. They rather bluntly utilize the mechanism of self-fulfilling prophecy.

There are others who seem to work hard to overcome their inner darkness, but as soon as a glimmer of light appears, they fearfully turn away from it and deny what they have seen. The rationalizations that usually follow—'I can't,' 'I don't have time,' 'I forgot'—only cloud the issue further.

The fear of being oneself is one of the greatest obstacles to be faced. This fear halts, hinders and deprives us more than almost any other challenge, if we allow it to.

It is not the drive for
growth to full realization
that is to be feared,
but the reluctance to overcome
the conditioning of infantile dependency
and chronic irresponsibility.

What to say then to the Fred within us? Calm down, be still and allow the real feeling and experience of Being to rise to awareness. Recognize the most precious force within you, the power to be. Honor that, live that, for that is your essence. Understand the fears for what they are and they will lose their power.

Dare to be!

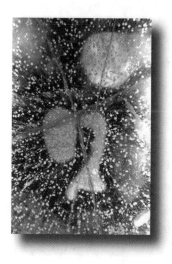

CHAPTER ELEVEN

IN QUEST OF THE HOLY MIRACLE

FIRST GLIMPSES

There once was a young man whose life experiences brought him closer to being in touch with his real Being. He found a guide through whom he gained most valuable teachings by which to lead his life to final fulfillment: he learned how to transform his experiences to lasting knowledge and wisdom regarding himself, his life and the world he lived in.

Through this guidance, glimpses of his life's significance emerged from the depth of his Being. He recognized that his innate clarity had been hidden under a thick crust of false conception which caused him to live in confusion, anxiety and self-negation.

With the help of his guide he learned to remove the veils that had covered, clouded and muffled his powers. Now the spring of his life promised to burst through the murky covering to find full expression in the light of unconcealed experience.

There were times when he glowed with the delight of the newly found self-discovery that pierced through his habitual state of confusion and uncertainty. Whenever he practiced the ways of true Being he had learned from his teacher, he experienced uplifting strength and clarity. The strength and clarity served as a contrast that accentuated the depressing weakness and turmoil he experienced whenever he returned to hiding in darkness.

In spite of the brilliance of these first experiences, the young man's long-standing attachment to the murky state stubbornly resisted his full involvement with clarity. A fierce struggle ensued between the habitual patterns that concealed his clarity and the recently awakened strengths that revealed it. Under the influence of his resistances, instead of using the guidance that had helped him grow, he sought to find fault with the very means that had brought about his awakening.

He polluted his sincerity by resorting to the dysfunctional behaviors of his past in addressing the process meant for growing out of them. He used this not only to negate his growth, but also his guide.

The young man sought to negate the guide through whom he had learned how to be self-empowered in clarity. Instead of seeking greater clarity, he sought argumentation.

Unbeknown by him, his arguments were as superficial as the murky mode of life they attempted to preserve. He bought his most obvious rationalizations.

The next step promoted by his resistances was to remove himself from the guide who had shown him how to tread the path toward clarity. Instead, he attached himself to a "famous master" who gave him "the touch of power."

THE PROMISE OF MAGIC

"Bring yourself to me," is the promise, "and by my special touch I shall transmit my power to you; troubles will be removed, struggles smoothed over"—how sweet seems the seduction.

An interesting array of self-proclaimed masters converge on the U.S.A., be it a perennial adolescent "saint" who promises, "Place yourself and your money into my hands and I'll do it all for you"; or a man who promises a secret and expensive crystal that will magically wipe away the necessity for individual responsibility; or any number of proponents of magic solutions that promise to free us of the necessity of doing anything for ourselves.

And not to neglect the host of sales personnel spawned within our culture who promulgate the seductions of fast-fix formulae that promise lasting change but deliver only the momentary sensations characteristic of pop-psychology. Numerous, indeed, are the merchants of disappointment.

Why do they attract such great numbers of followers in short periods of time? The most "successful" are the ones who carry the most extravagant promises of miraculous powers or of facile formulae.

The false teachers
prey upon the weaknesses in people
who have evaded facing themselves in truth,
and seem to find especially fertile ground
in our country
where gullibility and guilt
are easily played upon.

It is only logical that any of us who have not yet realized the fullness of our Being, have kept certain qualities of ourselves from being expressed, thereby preventing the experience of total Being. The human psyche cannot be at rest until every aspect of the individual is freely expressed; it will struggle unceasingly to overcome all suppressive factors.

It is just as certain that the suppressive factors, which, after all, have been in control for years, are not just going to lie down and say, 'OK, do it to me; wipe me out.'

The habitual patterns
that we instituted during our early years
to cope with life's challenges
now resist our inner urge
to foster our growth.

Hence the struggle that is familiar to everyone who has experienced internal growth. The quick-fix miracle merchants take advantage of any reluctance or fear to engage in this struggle.

The promises of easy miracle solutions, and the people who make them, can be extremely dangerous. They attract large groups of people, followers, who dupe themselves into believing they really want that—anything but the actuality of doing it themselves.

Such people mistakenly believe or hope they can rid themselves of the responsibility for their own fulfillment. They will seek out individuals who prey upon such weakness by promising to do everything for them. The promises often include some supposed magical formula or miraculous power by which all their troubles, their responsibilities and challenges, will purportedly be removed.

By such involvements we tend to avoid experiencing the beautiful reality of the striving, living and learning through which we can evolve toward true fulfillment. Attaching ourselves to false promises and false help, we sell our lives for a panacea, another illusion, instead of the crystalline clarity of the life that is ours. What a terribly poor bargain to strike!

Thus short-changed, we end up dedicating our feelings and thoughts—in fact our life—to rationalization instead of reason; we regress instead of progress. We attempt to convince ourselves that we have responded to the innermost urgings to honor our life, to experience and express life as it is, while we are actually enveloping ourselves even further in a life-choking cocoon of self-deception. This saps the essence out of the innate drive that tries to lead us toward real fulfillment, by diverting its energy into an illusory fad.

How could we make the fatal mistake of forsaking the experience of what is most precious about us, our life itself? By not remembering who we fundamentally and essentially are; by harboring misconceptions that identify us with self-limitation, isolation, weakness and lack.

No wonder our lives are then dominated by fear.

*Fear can drive us to commit
the most fatal and ironic mistake of all:
to forsake the experience of our life
for fear of losing it.*

Misconception, illusion and fear can be powerful foes; they nearly steal our life from us, like cancerous growths taking over our life force. But they also can be overcome.

THE WRESTLING MATCH

In your day-to-day efforts to grow toward fulfillment, you find that a wide array of energies compete for dominance within you. The familiar fights against the new and unknown; the pleasant seduces while the significant may repel; the limited promises security, while the infinite may convey a threat: these are aspects of your struggle with growth.

It is important to know that you can employ this very struggle as an instrument of the evolution in which you are engaged. The struggle is one of personal choices: discrimination and will versus blindness and helplessness. By means of this struggle you can effect your advancement.

We notice that in nature, growth seldom takes place in a straightforward line. Moments of advancement alternate with periods of rest and even apparent regression, just to yield to new surges of evolving energy.

We may frequently experience feelings of imbalance and fear just before we are about to evolve to a higher degree of consciousness. It is especially at this point that your resistances tend to be most powerfully aroused.

Through the process
of relating skillfully to your resistances,
you hone all your instruments and faculties
to fine sharpness and lasting strength,
empowering you to achieve
the beautiful balance
that characterizes attunement
with your true nature.

In light of this natural advancement, what a pity it would be to shrink from the process of growth when uncertainty appears.

If fear causes you to hold back,
you feel guilty.
To respond with guilt
when weaknesses are revealed,
is only to sidetrack into distraction
the energy inherent to real experience.

How much more fruitful it would be to face your recognition of internal turmoil with an attitude that says, 'Hmm, why is this happening? I remember from past growth experiences that they were preceded by imbalance, fear and resistance. New growth must be ahead, new realization. How interesting.'

The symptoms of resistance to growth
can serve as signals
that alert you
to the opportunity for growth.

With this attitude, imbalance, fear and resistance will not repel or arrest you. Instead you will relate to them as harbingers of growth.

It helps to know that once you face your resistances sincerely, with continuity and skill as well as with trust in yourself, their threatening power vanishes. Furthermore, you can learn to utilize your resistances to empower you toward the attainments they would otherwise oppose. You engage the energy inherent to them in purposefully achieving what they resist. You could call this "spiritual aikido": you welcome the opposing energy and use it to your advantage. When you consistently turn your resistances into signals of advancement, you become self-empowered. Therein lies your liberation.

You can look forward to the fresh directions of life's flow, even if you are somewhat frightened. To deny what you are experiencing would not serve you at all.

Every one of your experiences provides you with the opportunity to be aware that you are Being.

*It is the ultimate aim of every being to **be**,*
truly and to the fullest possible degree.

Thus you strive to experience every moment of life in undistorted consciousness. In such experience you discover the real miracle.

Life lies not
in the distant image of some perfect future,
but in the moment here and now.
It is through the struggle
toward balance and real experience
that life reveals and expresses itself.

Why would we wish to have someone take that away from us?

THE SWEETNESS OF LIFE

Imagine you were going on a mountain climb. Would your attitude be that you would prefer to be taken by helicopter to the top of the mountain, or would you rather overcome the challenges and obstacles of making the long climb on foot?

The first attitude may be held by those who are merely interested in the goal. The second attitude is characteristic of those who love the whole process of flexing their muscles, their skills and strengths, while overcoming challenges and savoring their experiences on the path. To them, the enjoyment of the mountain top is deeply enhanced by the experiences that brought them there.

Sometimes I ask our students, "If I were able to lift from you the struggle of life and do it all for you, how would you like that?" With rare exception the answer is, "No, I would not like that at all." One person said it quite succinctly: "Having someone else do it for me would take all the sweetness out of life." Of course that alone was enough to show her readiness to be responsible for her growth.

Yet we know that there are also those who think they would prefer it all to be done for them in some miraculous flash. They are afraid to own their process. Filled with fear, they would rather forfeit the beauty and excitement of their life process than face their fears or the possibility of failure.

Neither fear nor failure
need be awful or final
if you recognize them to be
just more experiences
by which you can grow
and consciously participate in Being.

Why trade all the fabulous intricacies of your own experience of evolution for a mere flashy phenomenon that purports to do it all for you? Why would anyone want that—even if it were possible?

Fortunately, life is infinitely too merciful to grant us every one of our wishes. The instant miracle solution is but a fantasy. The reality lies in the constantly recurring miracles of daily existence, of experiencing life, of simple Being.

CHAPTER TWELVE

THE STRESS RELEASE RESPONSE

Stress is a primary interference with the quest for fulfillment in contemporary society. On every level of humanity, from the man on the street to our leaders, stress contributes to tension and strife, thereby exacerbating the problems throughout the world. On a personal level, ineffective ways of responding to potentially stress-inducing situations can cause the erosion of our energy, susceptibility to illness and our general deterioration. Stress can seriously afflict and even shorten your life.

Thus it behooves you to consider the real causes, effects and cures for stress. Unfortunately, many of us confuse the causes of stress and therefore misdirect the intended solutions.

Let us examine how stress is caused. At the most basic level you are an energy system. You are composed of an intricate combination of balanced forces that coexist in continuous interplay. Among these interrelated forces are the instruments through which you experience and express your life. These instruments, your faculties, include the body and senses, the feelings, emotions, mind, intellect and intuition.

What do you experience when your forces are in harmonious balance? You experience an enjoyable and empowering sense of unified wholeness between your various parts, a sense of smooth cooperation. Their functioning is composed, effective and—at the same time—relaxed. The resulting sense of ease gives you pleasure and confidence. You are in touch with yourself at a deep level and look forward with calm enthusiasm to the experiences that life offers.

When you relate to life's offerings dysfunctionally,
with the unawareness and distraction
characteristic of being out of touch
with your real Self,
the delicate balance of your faculties
breaks down.

The result is a state of disharmony. Disharmony causes tension. The continued experience of unalleviated tension results in stress. Thus a cycle is created: inner dysfunction and self-neglect leading to imbalance followed by tension and then stress.

We usually blame circumstances and conditions for the stress in our lives. If circumstances and conditions were the cause of stress, all of us who are subject to potential stressors would suffer equally. However, we know that some individuals thrive under the possibility of stress, while others succumb to it. A problem to one person may be an opportunity to another. So, what makes the difference?

Stress is not caused
by circumstances and conditions
but by the way you respond to them.

Your adverse reactions to life's particulars cause stress, not the conditions and circumstances themselves. These reactions are founded upon a condition of being out of touch with your innate strength and ability. Let us eliminate this unfavorable response to potentially stressful situations.

You can count on challenges to be present in life. The potential for stress can be beneficial to you, if you know how to relate to it correctly. As an intelligent individual you make it a high priority to learn the effective ways by which you can use the energy inherent in stress to stimulate a positive proactive experience, rather than allow yourself to be a passive victim of the stress-inducing conditions.

You actually benefit from the challenges of life
that could be stress-inducing
by relating to them as reminders
to be attentive and nurturing to yourself.

It is the unfavorable response to the stress potential that causes us to break down and age prematurely, to suffer from such diseases as hypertension, heart disease and cancer. Unrelieved stress causes the breakdown of the integration between the various aspects of our Being. Our body and mind suffer from pain; their energy is blocked by tension. The pleasure, vitality and ease we experience in our natural state of unified wholeness and balance is replaced by a state of dis-ease. We have a contemporary term for this breakdown condition caused by unrelieved stress: "burnout."

The connections between stress and disease are no longer mere hypothesis; they are well established in fact. There is now a vast body of research and evidence showing stress to be a principal cause of illness, be it physical, neurological or psychological.

The reduction of stress has by necessity become a popular subject in our society. You can find innumerable superficial methods by which to address stress. To be really effective, how-ever, treatment for stress must come from your very core.

How do you do that? You must create a life strategy by which you permanently protect yourself from the harmful effects of the potentially stress-inducing situations in which you are so frequently immersed.

During the past thirty years I have worked with tens of thousands of students from many parts of the world on the ways of effectively reducing stress. These students include members of such high-stress professions as Hospice workers, doctors, lawyers, police officers, teachers and mothers. Among the most beneficial means of coping with stress, yielding predictably positive results, is the Stress Release Response™ developed at The Nataraja Yoga Ashram.

The Stress Release Response is a uniquely powerful and effective seven-step process that you can learn to implement at a moment's notice—as soon as you come upon a situation that would otherwise be stressful.

THE STRESS RELEASE RESPONSE

1. STOP
   Stop your heedless involvement with stress-inducing behaviors.

2. STEP BACK
   Broaden your perspective by viewing yourself beyond the immediate situation.

3. TUNE IN
   Become aware of yourself in terms of who you really are, including the strengths and abilities innate to you.

4. FOCUS WITH THE BREATH
   Use the rhythm of the breath to draw focused attentiveness toward your center.

5. COMPLETELY RELEASE
   Consciously release all tension from your body,
   emotions and mind.

6. EXPERIENCE
   Experience yourself in your enduring identity.

7. PROCEED IN FULL POWER
   Proceed in all moments, experiences and actions
   in the full power of who you really are.

Of course the full significance of each one of these steps
needs to be learned. Through learning the seven steps and
practicing them until they can be implemented at a moment's
notice, any sincere person can easily become free from the
tendency to react in a destructive way to potentially stressful
situations. This simple, but highly effective technique can free
you not only from the negative behaviors and effects that
usually come with stress, but also from the tendency to be a
victim of circumstances. This will ultimately empower you to
become more expert at leading your life to the fulfillment of
your potential.

CHAPTER THIRTEEN

HONORING THE POSITIVE

GROWTH AND LIBERATION

A lady who had been in one of my Expert In Life™ classes said to me, "Do you remember the conversation we had a few weeks ago? After talking to you, I gave up a number of misconceptions. I feel freer now—a burden I have carried for most of my life has been lifted. I am entering a new phase of development." I was glad to hear of her liberation and growth.

Then she told me, "I have decided not to continue with the next class, because I do not think I am ready." When I asked her why she felt unready, she said, "No matter what I try, I always end up the same; I never change. If I am to involve myself in this next class, it should be when I am ready to grow and change."

The contradiction is obvious, though the lady was quite unaware of it. How can she claim joy of having been relieved of a burden that she had lugged around for years—certainly a substantial change—and then state she never changes?

SLEIGHTS OF MEMORY

This magic trick is accomplished by a sleight of memory. We readily give credence to our weaknesses—our fear and anger and doubts, but forget or disregard our strengths—our ability to learn and laugh and grow.

A couple dissolving their marriage said in a session with me, "We have been married for exactly ten years and it has been downhill for nine years and eleven months." This attitude denies years shared in hope, child-rearing, family-forming and personal growth, not to mention the love in which they had initially united. To be sure, there had been conflicts, but there were also many moments of harmony. Why should the positive experiences be obliterated by the unhappy ones?

If you could choose between joy and sorrow, would you not choose joy? Not necessarily. You do have the choice, but your choice is determined by your attitude.

If your attitude is one of depression and pessimism, it will subtly, but persistently, color everything you experience with negativity. Similarly, if you approach life with a joyous, reality-oriented optimism, you may rest assured that your experiences will be positive and fulfilling.

Everything is interlinked by the law of cause and effect, which relates every action inexorably with its consequence. There is no reason why you should think that you, your attitudes and actions, are beyond the reach of this all-encompassing law.

We have the unfortunate tradition in our society of considering experiences of sadness, harshness or suffering as exclusive evidence of reality. "Life is a vale of tears and sorrow," we are told, "and to have an attitude of optimism is just unrealistic."

Listen to the exuberant song of birds on a bright spring morning, or the laughter of children at play, and then tell me about vales of tears and sorrow. Where now is your reality?

Experiences of joy, gentleness or flourishing need not be relegated to the realm of wishful thinking or fantasy.

Why should negativity,
which eats away at life's fabric,
be considered "realistic,"
while positivity,
which supports our experience of Being,
is derided as "unrealistic"?

A man looks at a photo of his face and muses, "Gee, I was a lot happier and more secure than I thought." Habitually, he considers it realistic to think of himself as being miserable, dissatisfied and agitated, even when he is not. What is the reality of his attachment to something that is not?

During a moment of wider perspective, this man can see that his usual perception of life is much more negative than his actual life. What good is it for him to undergo joyous moments, when he interprets and remembers them as sorrowful?

Even worse, soon after his more expansive perception, he will negate it by considering the photo of his happy face as "just a momentary accident," not as evidence of positivity in his life.

Habits have the nasty habit
of perpetuating themselves;
that is their nature.

LASTING IMPRESSIONS

Every experience you have—be it a thought, feeling or action—leaves an impression not only upon your brain, but on your entire neurological system, indeed, upon your whole person. These impressions tend to repeat the type of experience that formed them. Thus a negative thought will imprint upon you an impression that will tend to evoke further negative thoughts.

Negativity reinforces negativity.

This is not conjecture, but a neurological and psychological fact consistent with the law of cause and effect.

If negative experiences can form impressions of their kind —and there really is no "if" about it—then positive experiences must form positive impressions. Thus positive experiences can be consciously cultivated to cause further positivity.

THE FACT OF BEING

The reality of your existence
is that you are Being,
simply pure Being.

Whether you are happy or unhappy, poor or rich, young, old, sick or even lacking in consciousness, you still are: I am, you are, all is. Differences appear only in the degree and accuracy to which you experience and express Being. Being itself is constant and all-pervasive.

The Beingness that you are, persists independent of your physical and mental states. Viewed from the perspective of this life, you are still the Beingness at maturity that you were at infancy. You are constant Beingness, no matter how multiple are the changes in your body or mind.

Being is that which stands under all your experiences, whether you label them positive or negative. Thus, Being is your real substance, your essential nature. It is the one lasting aspect about you. Being is the permanency, the reality of you, unalterable by time, space, opinion, circumstance or condition.

Since Being is unalterable, it follows that Being is continuous.

After all the modifying layers
have been stripped away,
you recognize that you are
permanent, continuous Being.

There is then no realistic foundation in considering separate being. There is no such thing as "my being" or "your being" or "their being." All life forms, no matter how varied, are expressions of the continuum of Being, which transcends all limitations of time and space. No matter what kind of human being you are—intelligent, dumb, talented, wise, gross or subtle—you are still an expression of that continuum.

CULTIVATING POSITIVITY

When you base your thoughts, feelings and actions upon the continuity of Being, you generate impressions harmonious with your essence. As you progress within this harmony, a wonderful transformation occurs. You begin to be in fundamental agreement with yourself, to love yourself. Through this you learn to love your mate, children, friends, all humanity, indeed all life—for what is love but agreement with the essence of Being that we all are?

Accepting yourself,
you experience yourself as you are,
free from fear of unacceptability
and free of the desire to experience yourself
as other than what you are.
Thus you experience the fullness of Being,
not the emptiness of illusion.

Free of self-denial, you are also freed from the fear of spontaneous and unconditional experience of Being. Fear denies the freedom of Being; it binds you to self-limiting and negating habit patterns.

One may deny her learning, her growth, because she fears having to live by it. Another may negate his underlying state of happiness, fearing the responsibility of living in this state. The divorcee may want to forget the fine moments of her marriage and the good qualities of her husband in order to assign the responsibility for failure to anyone but herself.

We sometimes seem
more afraid of the positive
than the negative,
more afraid of success
than failure.

We may not remember the release and joy experienced during a session of yoga postures or meditation; we may habitually identify those positive practices with experiences of pain or frustration even if that was never the case. Otherwise everyone would continue in those beautifully balanced experiences and induce those deeply harmonious states that bring liberation.

The emotional gymnastics of denying our positive experiences result in the loss of a significant life process: learning. Such maneuvers do not alter reality, they only obscure our relationship to it.

How To Be

Free yourself from fearing or desiring what is not, and experience the fullness of life. Respect your learning, your achievements. Honor them, for they are the precious gifts of life. Welcome the plays of change as they occur, while remembering the permanence of Being. Remember to remember!

Appreciate the process of being; do not bury yourself in worries about goals. Experience yourself as you are. Then you will grow to fulfillment and embrace life in all its variety with real acceptance and respect: love. Let yourself be.

CHAPTER FOURTEEN

SELF-FULFILLING RELATIONSHIP

THE WANTING

Your life consists of a constant relationship with the people, conditions and objects that affect you. You want to relate to everything and all in such a manner that it yields fulfillment.

Let's face it: we all want. We want food and clothing and a roof over our head. We want to find a mate, or perhaps we want to escape the one we have. We want to feel good, to be healthy and happy. We want fulfillment.

> *There is not a creature alive*
> *who does not strive to be fulfilled.*
> *Indeed, this striving is an instrument*
> *that nature has instilled in all her creatures*
> *to serve her greatest aim: evolution.*

In human experience, the craving persists even when the basic necessities of food, clothing, shelter and procreation have been met many times over. Material comforts, social stability, emotional companionship and intellectual satisfaction cannot remove the gnawing yearning for more. We see proof all around us in the over-privileged who often suffer from greater need than their poorer fellow beings.

It seems that we cannot survive, let alone flourish, be happy and satisfied all by ourselves. We want to be related to the rest of the world and will not rest with satisfaction until we have achieved interconnectedness, unrestricted union. However, we make many mistakes in our relationships and thereby fail to fulfill what we seek.

Our relationships always involve more than one element: ourselves, and what we are relating to. Here we arrive at an oversight from which most of us suffer: we fail to consider ourselves as the fundamental element of the relationships we are involved in.

Without having established
a fulfilling relationship within yourself,
you cannot hope to successfully relate
to anyone or anything else.

GOODS AND SERVICES OR PEACE OF MIND?

The fulfillment we all seek is subtler than material wealth and less obvious than the superficial. Fulfillment is impossible to attain if we—through lifelong habit—reach out only for the tangible and obvious, neglecting the subtler essentials of life.

Most of us are so busily outward-directed
in our quest for satisfaction,
that we have neither the consciousness
nor the desire left
to be in touch with the inner Self,
who, after all,
is the one we are trying to fulfill.

It is astonishing how little real knowledge regarding ourselves we have. How can you fulfill someone whom you do not even know?

As a consequence, we find ourselves in the typical situation of working to acquire things in the mistaken hope they will satisfy us. Once they are gained, we work anxiously to protect and preserve them. Somewhat later, we recognize that their attainment did not fill the void within us. We are chronically disappointed and dissatisfied. Other people seem happier to us, and we envy them. Persistent anger, fear and sorrow complete this picture.

There is no law of nature that demands our bondage to such a negative state. If we were to overcome our misconceptions and re-channel our energy, we could free ourselves from the bonds of ignorance and illusion, from the slavery to overbearing sense-input and distracted mind. We could find fulfillment in the experience of a clear relationship to our real Being.

The intelligent approach is to establish the correct order of priorities and to live accordingly. This requires intimate and realistic knowledge of yourself, of the world you are a part of, and of the relationship existing between yourself and this world. Such knowledge, realistically implemented, results in your harmonious integration and successful relationship with all. This fully realized union is the ultimate relationship for which you yearn, consciously or unconsciously.

The person who knows that nothing but such an unlimited relationship will bring the desired condition of fulfillment, and therefore endeavors to achieve it, relates sincerely and fulfillingly to Self. The question is, are you capable of the deep knowledge that empowers you to relate to your life so fulfillingly?

SEEING THE LIGHT

During rare moments of clarity,
you find deep within your inner recesses
a reservoir of knowledge
which is so spontaneously understandable
that you recognize with certainty
the basic truth of those clear experiences.

For most of us, this experience of "seeing the light" does not occur often. We are usually so preoccupied by the insistent clatter of sense input and the meaningless meanderings of mind, that we blithely miss the signals of clear knowledge within. But, when at times of quietude and balance you are fortunate enough to tap into this inner knowledge, you experience a satisfaction so deep, and joy so full and lasting, that it transcends anything you can accumulate by amassing objects or by reaching "outside." You know then with certainty that you have touched something permanent and real in life.

You have connected with the real Self, your essence. This is described by the sages as the Silent Observer, the Impartial Witness.

Only when the Self is experienced
without intervening layers
of either desire or aversion,
of wanting or fearing,
is reality seen in clarity.

The opposing emotions color and confuse your vision according to their character. Their removal eliminates their effects. That is why real discrimination is one of the primary prerequisites of fulfillment. It takes a refined sense of reality to distinguish between that which merely appears to be pleasant and that which is truly good; between that which binds you to continued involvement with the superficial, thereby blunting your faculties, and that which frees you to plumb the depths of reality.

When your faculties
are in an effective relationship with you,
they serve you in making
the real and decisive distinction
between the false and the true,
the effects and the cause,
the illusory and the real.

Of all our faculties, the subtlest—and therefore the most finely pervasive in terms of truth—is the voice within. Your inner voice is comprised of the cumulative knowledge of all humanity as well as your accumulated experience as an individual.

The ability to be in touch with this inner voice—which is nothing but the voice of Self—is of paramount importance to the sincerely growing person. Such a person acts upon the profound new insights offered by the inner voice.

Responding to your internal knowledge is not as easy as it may seem. Formidable forces of opposite conditioning have to be overcome in order for you to honor the knowledge within. These conditioned patterns have been established in all of us.

The developing human being goes through the whole evolutionary process of nature. In the womb you grow from a single cell through various primitive stages until the infinitely complex infant is born. As an infant you operate on the most basic levels of existence, which initially differ little from those of an animal.

During the impressionable and defenseless stages of your formative years, you are incessantly assaulted by a barrage of influences from the outer world. These influences can cause you to react in predetermined ways that condition you to repetitive patterns of behavior. Thus, nearly indelible impressions are formed, binding you to the prevailing experiences of your grossest levels of existence.

WALLS FORCE YOU TO REACH HIGHER

With such prevailing conditioning and outer orientation, is it any wonder that the person who lives in harmony with the inner Self is rare indeed? There is so much to overcome; that is the challenge. The challenge is also your opportunity.

The current of opposition
becomes your opportunity
to rise to the highest realization:
in overcoming it,
you become stronger and more skillful.

You probably know from your own observations that it takes great courage to struggle against what seems so familiar and comfortable, no matter how erroneous it may be. Most people will opt for rationalizations, the self-deceptions which reinforce the artificial front and shut out the inner light.

The person who sincerely wants to integrate life with reality is aware of the all-too-human tendency to be lured into self-limitation by attachment to the familiar impressions formed in the past. When that awareness of our tendencies is consistently remembered, we can save ourselves from the trap of investing our energy in self-distracting guilt.

Sincerity is of the utmost importance in the quest for fulfillment.

You must determine
to see yourself as you are,
not as you wish to be or fear to be.

Yet how many people do you know who are so willing to face the unalloyed reality of anything, let alone themselves? But if your faculties are not in relationship to your real Self, what good are they to you?

Without the real-life experience of the inner depths—
wherein shines the light of true knowledge—there cannot be
psychological or spiritual health. The sincerely growing person
faces that fact of life, impresses it indelibly upon the memory
and relates to it consistently. That is fundamental to self-
fulfilling relationship.

A Bump Can Bruise Or Guide

Consistency is another indispensable factor on the path to
fulfillment in reality. It is a basic premise that reality is.

Just as you trip over stones
that you fail to see,
just as you bump into a wall
that you refuse to acknowledge,
so does reality remind you
of its constant presence
by little nudges, rude bumps
or painful tragedies,
according to what you require.
You can tune in to these helpful hints
and use their guidance
to not stray off the path.
For where does this path lead you—
but to the one fulfillment in reality
that we all seek...

We all have had experiences of losing sight of our relationship to reality, and we have suffered the consequent pain and
sorrow. With sincere determination any mistake can be turned
into a valuable learning experience. Any obstacle—no matter
how persistent—can be converted into a steppingstone to
higher realization.

We have no choice: we know our inevitable aim is fulfill-ment in reality. When you come to terms with that, you can find the energy within yourself to commit your life to a full relation-ship with the Being that you really are, no matter how long it takes and how difficult it is. No lasting peace or joy is possible without your union with reality.

You need not worry one bit about having to sacrifice any-thing in this quest other than illusion and its miseries. You do need to have the integrity to remain loyal to a positive commit-ment you have made to yourself. Thus integrity is of funda-mental importance. You order your choices so that all functions of life are properly and intelligently mobilized in service to your highest priority.

THE MENTOR AND WHY

There comes a time in your strivings when you recognize that it is quite unlikely you will always be able to referee the subtle, internal conflicts between the self-limiting ego and the limitless Self, between rationalization and right action. The secret and subtle wiles employed by ego to preserve its illusory supremacy are often beyond the range of the intellect.

Thus you will find, once you progress to subtler levels of experience, that a guide, a mentor, is necessary—one who has developed the delicate balance and keen inner eye required to traverse a bottomless gulf upon a razor's edge. In order to sub-vert your effort to reach the Self, the ego will try to convince you that you can cross over all turmoils into the state of full inter-connectedness on your own.

Once you determine to heed the true Self—the consciousness within—you will find a teacher in whom you can trust, a guide who has faced the truth within and knows it from direct experience. The teachings of such a person will awaken the knowledge of reality stored within your depth.

The real teacher
does not attempt to do your life for you,
but serves as the guiding light
toward the experience of the truth
residing within.

The true teacher will guide, but the student must be willing to place one foot in front of the other. The true teacher will enhance your strengths, point out your weaknesses, but will not coddle you by accepting responsibility for your fears, failings and self-deceptions. If you are sincerely determined to still the distraction, to hear the inner voice, you will eventually see the full import of your preceptor's teachings and recognize that those truths, and the truths in your core, are the same.

Then there arises from the depth of your heart the real experience of love, the harmonious realization of fundamental essence shared.

As a real student
you participate in a relationship
founded on equality, trust
and interconnectedness,
through which your internal powers
come fully to the fore.

With the ensuing surge of liberated energy, it becomes finally and fully possible to still the superficial clatter brought by ears, and hear the inner voice; to transcend the ephemeral image read by eyes and see beyond the momentary form; to overcome the one-dimensional input of senses and experience a fulfilling relationship with infinite reality. To this the true student of life resolves.

CONCENTRATION

CHAPTER FIFTEEN

CONCENTRATION: THE POWER BY WHICH YOU CLAIM YOUR LIFE

If we want to be fulfilled in life, we have to consciously choose what fulfills us and thereby stop occupying ourselves with what does not fulfill us. If we refuse to implement our conscious choice, we deserve what we get. We require a concentrated mind to successfully carry out our conscious choice.

To become adept at concentration, we need to understand some of the fundamental characteristics of mind. This understanding will be most thorough when we consider ourselves, the intended recipients of our mind's services, in fundamental terms.

The name by which we identify our species, human beings, indicates that we are Being, Being in human form. Thus the fundamental, and therefore the most important process that we are engaged in, is the experience of Being.

Everything about you
has as its fundamental function
your participation in either the expression
or the experience
of the fact that you are Being.

After all, what good would it be for you to be, if you were unable to experience or express it!

MIND: THE RELATIONAL INSTRUMENT

Your faculties—your body and senses, your feelings and emotions, as well as your mind, intellect and intuition—are the instruments by which you can consciously participate in being, on the many levels on which the Power of Being expresses itself.

Mind is the central correlating and coordinating instrument; it handles the activities of your faculties as they relate to the experiences and expressions of Being on all the various levels. However, your mind has some fascinating characteristics that can amazingly empower it or frustratingly derail it in its mission.

Human beings are thoroughly relational creatures; we experience our Being in relation to each other and the world we live in. Thus it is a characteristic of the human mind to be a relational instrument.

When you direct your mind
in the consciousness of who you really are,
your mind relates all experiences to you.
Thus you register the fullness of Being.

Your task, then, is to consciously direct your mind to relate all experiences to you as experiences of Being. Therein you find your ultimate satisfaction. When you fail in that fundamental task, your mind seeks satisfaction by absorbing itself in whatever object it happens to meet.

Relational instrument that it is, mind is then compelled to relate to any other objects to which the first object is related. I learned about this characteristic of mind from the Himalayan sage Krishnananda. This relational characteristic explains how your mind will wander willy-nilly from one object to another in continuous succession when it is not consciously directed.

Mind's wandering from object to object is somewhat similar to the flight of a spaceprobe. Do you remember the spectacular flight of the Voyager, the first human-made object ever sent out of the solar system?

Voyager accomplished this feat by flying to a planet, rotating partially around it and utilizing the energy of that involvement to propel itself like a slingshot toward the next planet where it would repeat the procedure. Who knows how long that will continue?

The problem with mind going from the experience of object to object is that you are usually not consciously involved with those flights of your mind. You, the intended recipient of those experiences, are left out. This is the classical distraction from which we suffer.

As the owner of a habitually distracted mind, we suffer the effects of the mind's absence from us. This ultimate absent-mindedness deprives us of the deeply satisfying sense of focus and purpose in our life; it has us feeling adrift, deprived and full of fear; we complain of experiencing a sense of inner void.

So here is this wonderful characteristic of our mind—to be an instrument of relationship—that has been misused after having fallen into the wrong hands, so to say, because the rightful owner has not consciously claimed its services.

When you do not appropriate your mind unto yourself by relating its experiences consciously to the Being that you are, all mind's relationships are dysfunctional; your life is dysfunctional.

THE SHAPE OF MIND

Your mind does not really have a mind of its own. The mind is not a discreet entity; it is not any kind of organ or object; it is a subtle form of energy.

Mind has the curious characteristic of taking on the attributes of whatever it relates to. The ancient seers were fond of the analogy of molten metal.

> *As molten metal poured into a crucible*
> *takes the shape of that crucible,*
> *so does the mind take on the "shape"*
> *of the object it is involved in.*

If, for example, you are thinking about a tree, your mind becomes absorbed in the shape of that tree; if you are thinking about Being, your mind reflects to you the characteristics of Being.

LEARNING CONCENTRATION

Now it is easy to see why we want to be in charge of mind's involvements. It is important to focus our mind on a chosen point. We keep it fixed there so it does not go willy-nilly from one object to another. Having our mind remain steadily involved with a chosen object, be it a thought, a concept or any other conscious experience, is highly beneficial and deeply satisfying to us.

We can learn to withdraw mind from its habitual outward-going patterns. This withdrawal from distraction allows us to gather our mental energies and fix the mind at will upon a chosen point. That is concentration.

I assume that you want to be clear and focused as you go through life. However, from your own experience you know there are many circumstances, conditions and objects that can distract us even from the experience of what is most important about us, the fundamental fact that we are. Then we also miss out on the expression and enjoyment of Being. Distracted from the fundamental, our life is severely limited.

Concentration is a skill that has to be learned and cultivated if we want to lead our life to fulfillment and success. To develop the skills and powers of concentration, you first cultivate awareness of mind's habitual workings by the practice of silent observation. You adopt the attitude of witnessing whatever transpires in your mind without judging or interfering. You will be surprised by the depth of calmness and clarity that such a simple practice can provide.

Next you train mind to remain focused on a chosen point at will. Sincerely and repeatedly, you practice keeping mind fixed on that point alone. This point can be something as simple as a geometric design, or a flower, the flame of a candle, your breath or the area of your heart, which you may relate to as your center. The latter two are focal points I personally like to recommend for the simple reason that they are always accessible to us.

Once you have strengthened mind's ability to remain focused on a chosen point, it is able to focus at length on any other point. Now mind is ready to perform the essential function for which it was created.

PARTICIPATING FULLY IN BEING

*Mind's fundamental function
is to participate fully
in the experience and expression
of the Being that you are.*

Mind is now ready for the ultimate application of its special ability to take the shape of its object: mind takes the shape of Being. Those who know of the infinitude of Being will understand the magnificent ramifications of such a state.

Just think of how wonderful it would be to have your mind steadily fixed on what is most important and pleasurable to you: the experience of Being. What expansive joy you would experience! You could realize a satisfaction far beyond anything you have ever even imagined…

When mind is steadily fixed,
by will,
on the Being that you really are,
that is meditation.

You can so transform your mind and all your faculties that you live in the state of meditation constantly and dynamically, whether you are at rest, work or play. Then you remain in the utterly calm and tranquil experience of abiding peace. Therein lies fulfillment.

Concentration is the power by which you withdraw mind from its habitual outward-going patterns and gather mind's strength into a wholeness of great power. You can then overthrow the dictatorship of self-limiting modes of thinking, feeling and acting. By the power of concentration you claim the life that is yours to live and lead—to fulfillment.

CHAPTER SIXTEEN

EXPERIENCING THE
PLEASURE OF CONCENTRATION

You are Being.
Being is to be experienced.
In the conscious experience of your Being
you fulfill the real purpose of your life.

You are constantly seeking fulfillment. The only way you can ever have fulfillment is by being true to your purpose. You are true to your purpose by experiencing yourself as you are, in reality, free of distortion and free of distraction.

The most direct way to a fulfilling experience of the reality of your Being is concentration. Concentration is the state in which all the resources through which you experience and express your life are harmoniously united and focused. Without concentration your life passes you by while you do not even know that it is happening. That is a profound loss to suffer.

Thus it behooves you to learn everything you can about concentration. The greatest teacher is direct experience.

Since your mind performs such a central function in relation to the activities of your faculties, concentration involves mind in a specific way. In the concentrated state, you focus your mind at will upon a chosen point. It is the fundamental purpose of your mind to be focused upon the total experience of Being.

When the mind is steadily focused, your other faculties—emotions, feelings, intellect and intuition, and even body and senses—become part of that focused state. This state yields a beautiful experience of balance, comfort and clarity.

Let us open ourselves right now to a simple and direct experience of concentration.

Place your body in a comfortable position in which it can remain effortlessly balanced, without having to involve mind with adjusting the body. Purposefully tell your body to relax deeply now, and release all tension.

When your faculties are in a deeply relaxed state, they allow you to concentrate more effectively. You will be rewarded if you focus sincerely for a few moments on telling the major parts of your body to relax.

It works well to focus on one part of the body, tell it to relax, feel the relaxation flowing through that part, and then move on to the adjacent part. You progress like this in a continuous flow until the whole body is deeply relaxed.

Sincerely done, this process helps you to withdraw mind from its habitual enmeshment with outgoing tendencies and prepare it to focus upon a point of your choice. You can choose as an initial focal point the simple act of observing your own breath.

So, right now, steadily engage your mind in observing the breath. Every time you inhale, have your mind trace the flow of breath as it enters through your nostrils and goes into your lungs. Your mind will quite naturally be led to the general area of your heart.

Imagine the area of your heart to be your center. Simply consider your mind to be resting with effortless balance in your center.

Let every breath remind you to keep your mind absorbed in your center. After resting steadily in the center for a while, your mind feels more at home here. It becomes calm, tranquil, deeply at peace. Remain relaxed. During every breath and every moment, now, allow your mind to rest quietly in your center.

Every time you inhale, let your mind experience your center and reflect that center as being wide open, indeed limitless, free of all boundaries.

As you exhale, experience your center free of obstacles, disturbances and constrictions.

Inhale and let your mind witness your expanding toward infinity.

Exhale and experience yourself clear of all negativity.

Keep using your breath as a reminder, so that your mind does not go wandering off into distraction.

You are now helping your mind to overcome distractions, not by fighting them, but by simply staying involved with a positive and deeply pleasing point of focus.

When your mind is steadily present and centered,
it easily becomes aware
of the experience of Being,
of the simple fact that you are.
That experience, when continuous and at will,
is called meditation.

Thus, concentration can yield meditation.

In the experience of Being there is deep pleasure, great satisfaction. Only when your mind has the experience of Being as its focus, can you experience the fulfilled state you have always yearned for.

So cause every breath to serve as a reminder. Keep centered. Visualize your center to be in the area of your heart. Train your mind to be totally at ease, completely relaxed here.

With sincere and repeated practice, you will find it easier and easier to keep your mind steadily focused in your center. Your mind will feel deeply secure and at home here. Now concentration is not a struggle for your mind, but a pleasure.

Feel arising within yourself a sense of calmness and steadiness. You are released from worries, tensions and negativity— feeling dynamic, balanced, confident.

Allow your mind to be clear as you remain focused on your center with every breath. Mind is growing stronger, deeply at peace.

Now, in your center, you can experience the light of consciousness, the awareness of Being. Rest in that.

The clear mind
reflects the undistorted experience
of simple miraculous Being to you.
Here you find the fulfillment
of all needs and desires.
You abide in the peace
that your life has always been striving for.

When you remain focused in this balanced presence, you meet life's situations with equanimity and clarity. You relate every action that you engage in, indeed every breath you take, to this concentrated consciousness, and thereby experience the wholeness of your life's fabric.

In this way, the fulfillment of your existence is revealed to you; it is revealed in every event, every experience and every moment. Life makes sense.

THE MIND
AND ITS PATTERNS

CHAPTER SEVENTEEN

TURNING OBSTACLES INTO STEPPINGSTONES

DEPENDENT VICTIM OR SELF-EMPOWERED VICTOR?

The human being has an innate yearning for freedom. We chafe under the dictatorship of circumstances that hinder us, conditions that limit us and people who impose upon us. We feel oppressed by any self-limiting patterns of thoughts, feelings or behaviors: they interfere with the full expression of our Being. Until we feel free, we cannot be at peace.

Many people think, feel and act as if their life were dictated by circumstances and conditions. They feel tormented by the slavery that they think is imposed by those contingencies. As a consequence such individuals feel dependent and helpless, therefore disempowered and not responsible.

However, it is no secret that there are innumerable situations that are deemed terrible by some and wonderful by others. For example, a person caught in a rain shower may react to the rain with despair, while a child delights in the same situation. Getting fired from a job is devastating to some individuals, while others view it as an opportunity to move on to something better. The documented instances of individuals becoming better persons from the hardships suffered in prisoner-of-war camps are well known.

The difference
between being a victim
and a victor
is the internal attitude
by which you regard yourself.
If you regard yourself as dependent
upon circumstances and conditions,
you will predictably live as a victim;
if you regard yourself as self-empowered,
you will live as a victor,
transcendent to circumstances and conditions.

Real independence from circumstances and conditions takes place only when you relate to events and situations as ways of experiencing that you are. Furthermore, your experience of the fact that you are, needs to be based upon thinking of yourself in terms of your fundamental identity, the Power of Being. Thus we can note again the importance of the way our mind relates to us.

MIND AND CONSCIOUSNESS

Mind is the principal instrument with which you relate to the circumstances and conditions of the world around you and within you. Your mind is not a physical organ, but a powerful and subtle energy system that performs your thinking and psychological processes.

Central to all those experiences is the awareness of yourself. Self-awareness is called consciousness.

It is of fundamental importance for you to relate consciously to your experiences in and of the world, to relate them to the awareness of yourself. The central medium through which much of this relating takes place is, again, the mind.

While mind is not a material object,
it is affected by matter.
You could visualize mind
as an intangible movie screen
upon which
the experiences of the tangible world
are projected.
These projections are taken in
by the conscious Self
in self-experience.

This analogy, however, is only partial. Unlike the movie screen, mind is not a passive object. The mind is an intangible constellation of energy that correlates, among other things, the input of the senses.

The senses relate to the material, the tangible world, which is also the grossest and most limited level of existence. Through its involvement with the senses, mind may become entangled with the material level to such an extent that it has minimal involvement with the other levels of existence.

Thus we become deprived of the rich subtleties of life and lose the experience of the fullness of Being. Our consciousness, the limitless experience of real Being, then seems clouded and limited.

Consciousness is intangible like mind, but unlike mind, it is limitless. Infinitely subtle and all-pervasive, consciousness cannot be experienced by the senses, for they are limited by their involvement with matter. Not even the mind can experience the limitlessness of consciousness.

Consciousness can be experienced
only by consciousness.

Consciousness, the awareness of Being, is the basis of all your awareness of yourself as a feeling, thinking, living being. Without consciousness you could not be.

THE DISTRACTED MIND

Mind, not a material medium, is fundamentally of the nature of consciousness. Yet mind is different from consciousness. While consciousness is the awareness of Being in totality, mind usually occupies itself with the partial.

Mind correlates fact and fiction, solves problems or meanders meaninglessly. Additionally, much of mind's energy is absorbed in handling sense data, which is relatively gross, unsubtle and fragmentary. All these activities tend to take the place of full consciousness, the experience of the fullness of Being that you are, which mind is meant to reflect. You can see now how your mind can be fragmented and thereby distracted.

Mind's tendency toward distraction combines with another important characteristic of mind: it can handle only one thing at a time. We may think we can drink our tea, read the paper and commune with our mate at the breakfast table all at once, but in fact, our little mind is nimbly jumping from one activity to the other in amazingly rapid succession. This characteristic can lead to further fragmentation.

We have explored how mind has the curious characteristic of taking on the attributes of whatever it relates to. In conforming like the chameleon, mind does not discriminate. If one little fragment is before the mind, then mind becomes like that one little fragment. If multiple minuscule fragments of reality are related to by the mind in rapid succession—as usually is the case—then mind will rapidly assume the shape of multiple

minuscule fragments. No wonder we experience so much fragmentation, distraction and clutter.

What happened to the well-rounded and fulfilling
experience of the wholeness of Being? Gone.

THE FOCUSED MIND

To rescue yourself from the sorrowful fate caused by fragmentation and distraction, you have to call upon the same
characteristics of mind that can be such hindrances, and turn
them into aids. If your mind does not discriminate, who will?
You must.

Instead of allowing mind
to take on the characteristics
of innumerable disparate fragments,
concentrate your mind
on the full meaning of your life:
the clear and true experience of Being.
Cause mind to be so absorbed
in the experience of the Being you are,
that your mind merges with,
and takes on the shape of Being.

No matter how many obstacles—or opportunities—life
presents to you, keep your mind focused on the simple
experience of the fact that you are. In this manner every
experience, no matter how great an obstacle it may first seem to
be, can be related to as an experience of Being and thus bring
you closer to fulfillment.

In learning to become expert at leading your life, your mind
naturally develops the positive habit of turning obstacles into
steppingstones toward fulfillment. Thus you develop and
consistently assert your independence over circumstances and
conditions that would otherwise take over your existence.

You are right now. That is not difficult to know, but deeply significant. Absorb mind in the experience of Being with full sincerity and continuity. From moment to moment simply and sincerely cause mind to reflect the fundamental fact that you are.

With proper practice, mind will take on and reflect the characteristics of your true Being: luminous, calm and secure, abiding in the balanced joy of unencumbered Being. In essence, self-knowing Being is what we all are. To be in the experience of self-knowing Being is real fulfillment.

CHAPTER EIGHTEEN

EXPERIENCING CLEAR REFLECTION WITH A CALM MIND

A wonderful fact about our mind is that it is able to reflect Being to us with such clarity and fullness that we can be flooded with the most joyous and fulfilling experience—experience which gives us such a wealth of lasting insight and satisfaction that our whole life is enriched.

Imagine you are on a walk high in the mountains and you have never seen the sun in your whole life. You come upon a beautiful tranquil mountain lake. Its surface has neither ripple nor wave, just crystal-clear reflection.

The unruffled water reflects the sun as a perfect orb, so free of distortion that you can know what the sun really looks like. Additionally, your gaze penetrates easily to the very depths of the silent lake where wonderful secrets of life are clearly revealed.

In your imagination, cast a pebble into the lake. You see immediately a modification taking place: the previously smooth, reflecting surface of the lake is disturbed by wave after rippling wave emanating from the initial point of impact. The reflection of the sun has been broken into so many fragments that the image of the orb is no longer recognizable.

If the lake's condition were to be modified by an even stronger force, say a windstorm, the churning waves would upheave the very bottom and muddy the deepest waters. Only when the disturbances cease and the waters become still again, will you be able to gaze into the depths of the lake. When not a ripple distorts the surface, you are able to see the true reflection of the sun again.

Your mind, like the mountain lake, is a reflecting medium. In its pure state it has the calm clarity to reflect your Self as well as your life experiences to you, free of distortion. Any other state of mind can be considered a modification.

When, for example, your mind involves itself with outside objects, without making them part of the experience of the Being that you are, your mind is in a state of modification.

*Because your mind's original purpose
is to reflect to you the experience of Being,
any mental state which distracts you
from that most important experience
is a modification.*

The modifying factors are innumerable and they constantly assault your mind with their powerfully distracting and distorting influences. Unchecked, they churn your mind into a state of imbalance and turmoil. Your experience of life becomes so fragmented as to be unrecognizable and confusing. The clarity and depth you experience with the undisturbed mind is replaced by the turbulent muddiness characteristic of the modified mind.

Remember that mind's true function is to serve your consciousness, your awareness of Being.

Though your mind can be a focusing force
toward ultimate success and fulfillment,
it can also be
your greatest source of distraction.

In the unchecked, modified state, your mind can behave like a drunken monkey—reeling from one thing to another in such rapid succession that you do not know whether you are coming or going. Under the influence of a distracted mind you even forget to tune in to the fact that you are Being. For all practical purposes, it is to you as if you were not existing. What a waste of what is most precious about you: the fact of your Being!

The ensuing turmoil can easily eat up more energy than a day of hard labor. If you often find yourself utterly exhausted, it may very well be due to the turmoil and energy drain caused by the incessant modifications of your mind.

Most of us suffer much of the time from such distraction. We are so thoroughly conditioned into the distracted state that we tend to accept it as normal. In the state of distraction lies our suffering and failure.

Unfortunately, many of us attempt to escape the painful and humiliating experience of missing our life in distraction by distracting ourselves even further. When depressed, we eat or go shopping irrespective of need. When bored, we seek titillation of the senses rather than being attentive to ourselves in our life. These behaviors only compound the error and increase our pain.

Fortunately there is an inherent drive
deep within you
that always guides and prods you
toward your liberation from the hindrances
which limit your experience of Being:
the drive toward realization of the true Self.
Responding to the drive toward Self-realization
empowers you to grow toward your fulfillment.

It is by calling upon this inner drive that you find the strength and skill to create a center of calm clarity within your-self, no matter how chaotic and demanding the inner challenges and outer world may be.

There is no doubt that the internal and external conditions which beset us can be extremely destructive to our health and hopes, but it is even more certain we contain within ourselves all we need to rise above conditions, and live true to the Being we really are.

CHAPTER NINETEEN

BREAKING THE DICTATORSHIP OF IMPRESSIONS HABITS AND COMPULSIONS

Do you remember times when you really wanted to apply your mind to solving a pressing problem and your mind just would not cooperate? Sometimes it seems that when we need it most, mind wanders everywhere but where we need it.

Our mind can be so enmeshed
in an intricate network of distractions
that we feel as powerless
as a bound prisoner.

This can be an extremely frustrating situation. The distracted mind, instead of serving us, enslaves us.

None of us wants to be helplessly caught up in the clutches of our mind's distractions. We want to be able to use our mind for our purposes, and to apply its full force to any chosen point. To free ourselves from the entanglements of a distracted mind, it is important for us to understand a major characteristic of mind.

We know that our brain, which is the seat of our mind, has convolutions etched into it by our experiences. Similarly our mind, like a malleable matrix, has each of our experiences impressed upon it. Future experiences will tend to be added to and deepen the previously established impressions.

Visualize a brand-new mountain spring beginning its journey toward the sea. The first water meanders down the mountain, going left and going right, seeking its way past obstacles, all the while forming a subtle impression upon the ground it travels. The waters that follow naturally tend to flow along the impressions formed by the initial trickle. As more and more water flows, the impressions are cut deeper and deeper into the earth, until there is a great river forging through the canyons it has worn into the rocks and even into the mountains.

Like so many other things in nature, our mind tends to take what appears to be the path of least resistance, especially if left to its own devices. This tendency is the underlying cause of the principle of impressions.

In infancy, your initial experiences are impressed upon a matrix as smooth as a ball of clay. We even speak of how impressionable children can be.

Each impression carries within itself the latent power to evoke another experience similar to the one that caused the initial impression. Thus your actions are compelled to follow each other as do the waters in the stream. This means the impression will be made deeper and deeper. The potential of that impression to re-evoke experiences of its kind increases with each repetition.

This explains how it has come about that many of our actions are directed by habit patterns. As these habits are allowed to persist, they continue to form their impressions even deeper.

We find ourselves falling into the same patterns of behavior over and over again. We aptly describe this as "being in a rut."

The persistent demands of deeply etched impressions can be so ruthlessly dictatorial that they tend to take over our life and our experience of ourselves within it. Many of our actions are then determined by compulsions.

The very faculties that we value
for contributing to our humanness—
our ability to discriminate and choose,
our free will—
are usurped by automatic patterns
that engage us in modes of behavior
contrary to our satisfaction and welfare.
In those modes of behavior
we seem condemned
to a life of limitation and frustration.

It is our good fortune that we really are not so helpless. For while negative tendencies do exist in every one of us, we also have the power to contradict them. When you recognize that your mind is caught up in negative habit patterns, you can summon the energy within yourself to purposefully withdraw mind from those patterns.

If you were to find your hand touching a hot stove, you would quickly withdraw it. Similarly you want to react quickly and withdraw your mind from harmful habit patterns.

If you find you are lacking in that quick reaction, you can train yourself by practicing behaviors which are beneficial to you, such as yoga, meditation and other positive ways of being. Through such practices you can simply and effectively withdraw mind at will from any involvement that is contrary to the full and clear experience of your real Being. This is an indispensable step to your liberation.

CHAPTER TWENTY

INDUCING A STATE
OF POSITIVE POWER

A life that relates all aspects of the individual realistically and harmoniously with the multifarious conditions of our total environment is the ultimate aim of all instincts, needs and desires. All actions performed by the various life forms throughout nature strive fundamentally toward the fulfillment of these drives.

Life is characterized by movement. Movement aims at balance. The state of equilibrium allows for the full experience of oneself in harmonious relationship with all the factors comprising the situation, i.e. with reality.

Reality is that which—
independent of our self-deceptions,
rationalizations, little white lies
and gross misrepresentations—
is the real condition
of the workings of the universe.

145

Reality will not be disproved by changes or time, as it is ultimately independent of conditions. Reality always and unconditionally just is.

When you recognize reality and live in accord with it, you experience the grand workings of nature within and about you. All your faculties function then knowingly, joyously and harmoniously in realistic relationship with your total Being. Denial of reality or attempts to change, twist or bend it by calling events or objects by a different name, result in pain similar to that experienced when we say a wall is not a wall and walk nose-first into it.

We do not always purposely set ourselves against reality. We are conditioned by a lifetime of experience into self-limiting habits of behavior—patterns of feeling, thought or action which lead to distortion and confusion. In the face of their persistent clamor we find it difficult, if not impossible, to experience existence in calm clarity.

When we learn to quiet this demanding clamor, we can use the far finer and more expansive powers of our faculties to experience a significantly fuller, wider and more functional— therefore more realistic—view of what is.

> *To know reality in fullness*
> *is to live truly.*
> *True recognition of reality*
> *means merging with it.*
> *Knowing it and being it are one.*
> *Truly being means really being,*
> *which ultimately is what*
> *existence is all about.*

We now face our need to relate truly to reality, but have extreme difficulty employing the faculties needed to give us the deep and wide-ranging perception characteristic of that experience.

Your life is fashioned by your thoughts and the actions that result from them. These experiences are impressed upon your neurological system like grooves upon a recording disc and are strengthened by repetition. Thus habits are formed. Habits form your character, which in turn is a decisive factor in the molding of your destiny.

You know if you give poisonous food to your body, it suffers, disintegrates. To overcome ill effects, you ingest food that is in harmony with the basic constituents of your body, thereby building up the positive strength of the body.

Thoughts are vibrations
that radiate their influence like waves
throughout your Being.

If you habitually induce false concepts—ideas disharmonious with reality—you are introducing disruptive vibrations to your Being. The structure through which your Being is expressed will then tend to disintegrate. You will experience through your faculties such symptoms as tension, frustration, hatred, anger, pain and sorrow, instead of the underlying reality of harmonious integration. If you let these symptoms continue unchecked, they will evoke more of their kind, making them the predominant modes of vibration you experience.

To introduce healthy reality-oriented patterns of vibration to your faculties, and to strengthen them by repetition, can now be seen as a direct means to positively affect your life. We know from the ancient sages as well as from contemporary science, that the essential constant of all existence is energy. Energy is manifested as vibration. Thus to harmoniously relate and align your faculties to a clear vibratory state, to the essential state, is a direct inroad to the positive self-motivation and Self-realization you seek.

There are specific sets of powerful, positive vibrations you can utilize to evoke vibrations akin to your essential nature, radiating their harmonious effects throughout your Being and beyond. These concentrated vibrations in the form of words are called "mantras."

Mantras are the pure vibrations of positive qualities inherent to the universe. The repetition of mantra correctly learned is an exact science. Through correct mantra repetition, you can actively reinforce positive impressions upon your brain and nerve channels, upon your intellect, mind and body—as well as your actions—until you flow habitually in those positive patterns.

By expertly availing yourself of the power of mantra, you burn out mind's dross. You eliminate disturbances, dissipations and distractions while the pure vibratory modes evoked by mantra take over, bringing balance and equability. You notice that you feel better about yourself, more confident, clear and strong. You recognize the goodness of what, how and who you essentially are. You learn to accept, appreciate and love yourself—and thereby others.

The positive effects of consciously creating an empowered vibratory state penetrate deeply into all levels. No longer do you derail yourself or injure yourself by clumsy accidents. You feel more energetic and alert. Powers of concentration increase tremendously. You work more efficiently and joyously. Relationships become deeper, more real.

Mantras properly applied
align you realistically with what is
and attune you
to the free flow of your full potential.

It can be a source of great confidence and power for you to realize that you need not regard yourself as a helpless victim of established circumstances. You need not be a slave of the past, but can claim your self-empowerment. In this way you realize your ultimate independence from circumstances and conditions. Through this you can make real your liberation.

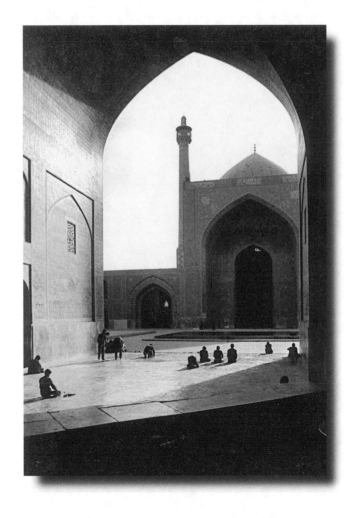

MEDITATION

CHAPTER TWENTY-ONE

THE EMINENTLY PRACTICAL APPROACH TO A SUCCESSFUL AND FULFILLING LIFE

For our life to make sense, for it to be successful, satisfying and fulfilling, we have to experience it in full consciousness.

The conscious participation in your existence,
from moment to moment,
with the harmonious integration
of all your faculties, at will, is meditation.

That is the state our life is always striving for, the experience that our ambitions and desires, our aspirations and drives are always aiming for, whether we know it or not.

Often we do not experience the moments and events of life in conscious relation to ourselves. As a result, we can feel emptiness, a sense of something lacking and even boredom while our life is filled with activities.

This state perplexes us. We think we are doing well, working hard, so, why are we not happy, not satisfied? Unless we derive the solution, we will eventually become demoralized.

When we do not know what our real life goal is, our priorities become confused.

The fulfillment of your potential
in clear, conscious experience
is your only and ultimate fulfillment;
it is the meaning and reason
of every one and all your actions,
from the simplest breath
to the most complex undertaking.
It is your highest priority.

We do so much and work so hard throughout life to find fulfillment. Unfortunately, we often get sidetracked and stuck in states which give us such limited satisfaction that it is no satisfaction at all. That is frustration.

The full experience of Being,
in the awareness
of the harmonious integration
of all your aspects,
is meditation.

That is the ultimate in well-being, in health. We tend to think of health only in terms of our body, or sometimes in terms of our mind, but seldom in terms of our fully balanced system of forces.

When we tend to the health of one part at the expense of the others, the others will suffer and pull the favored aspect down with them. The powerfully balanced state of ease we experience in meditation gives way to dis-ease when we abandon that balance.

Disease and stress are the actions within or upon a balanced system of forces which result in the deformation of that balance. Unrelieved stress results in the exhaustive destruction of the entire system. This is what we bring about when we do not keep our priorities in their proper order.

We can be so bent on satisfying our body's demands that our mind becomes exhausted and dulled; we can coddle ourselves in such emotional indulgences that our body becomes depleted, mind short-circuited, intellect excluded and intuition neglected; we can lose ourselves in such mental distraction that all is forgotten, including the fact that we are.

There is really no pleasure in such self-limiting or even self-destructive modes of being. Running after momentary, partial pleasures while neglecting the experience of the all-inclusive and lasting pleasure, just does not make sense. There is absolutely no advantage to it.

Inherently, we cannot rest, cannot be at peace with ourselves and our life when we are not in the consciously integrated experience of the Being that we really are. What does it serve us to spend our life energy running after objects of pleasure when we are too distracted to be aware of the fact that we are existing?

What benefit is it to us when we involve ourselves in relationships which so blind us that we cannot even relate them to our existence—which we have forgotten all about? What good would it be for us to have a grand gourmet feast and wolf down the food so fast that we could not even taste it?

Meditation is
the conscious and balanced involvement
in the experience of Being
that allows you to fully savor every moment.
You learn to integrate and appreciate
every circumstance, condition and event
as yet another texture and color
on the limitless canvas that is your life.

Far from being a discipline to be imposed upon us, meditation is the direct means to our fulfillment. Meditation is not some strange theoretical practice; it is the most natural and direct state of being. Meditation is not a distant dream, but the eminently practical approach to a successful and fulfilling life.

CHAPTER TWENTY-TWO

MEDITATION
WHY ISN'T EVERYONE DOING IT?

Meditation is the simple and beautifully clear experience of existence in calm continuity, balanced ease and self-knowing awareness. It is the most deeply satisfying state that we can be in. Intrinsically, we all want to live in such a wonderful experience of pure Being. So, why don't we?

There are aspects in each of us that are not at all accustomed to that state. Have we not been habituated to a life so opposite, a life so distracted and scattered by our outer functioning and inner turmoil that the pure act of being seems quite unfamiliar to us? That is why we have to spend so much time talking about and attempting to gain what we already are: we are Being.

The mere fact that we are not accustomed to living in the joy of full awareness of ourselves does not mean that we cannot. When we feel inner stirrings in that direction, we must neither disregard them, nor dismiss ourselves as incapable or unworthy of such wonderfully alert and alive experience. Rather, we could passionately assert our awareness that we are intrinsically capable and deserving of such fulfillment. We acknowledge our potential and sincerely determine to realize it by directing our behaviors and actions accordingly.

What are we to do? We yearn for the experience of genuine Being; we need it, yet have difficulty approaching this most simple, direct and healthy way of being. Although we know deep within that it is an utterly natural and universal experience, it may seem foreign to us. Meditation is the answer and it is available to all of us.

> *Meditation does not belong to a select few;*
> *it belongs neither to yogis nor to the East.*
> *It is the conscious realization*
> *of the Being we all are,*
> *experienced in clarity,*
> *spontaneity and continuity,*
> *at will.*

That is meditation. And that is all it is.

Now, sometimes we have to watch our motives. Granted, here is the simplest, most naturally fulfilling state of being that every human being of all times and cultures innately wants. Yet few of us are in that state. Most of us plead ignorant of its existence or possibility. Why?

> *In our predominant tendency to go outward,*
> *we have become conditioned*
> *to seeking our happiness in other beings,*
> *other objects and conditions.*

We have spent most of our life and energy in that pursuit. We are deeply oriented in the outward direction. It seems difficult for us now to change course, even while knowing that we have to if we want to make any sense out of our life at all, which we do.

The old habit patterns demand to remain in charge. They want to waylay our efforts to be clearly, calmly conscious in the experience of the present moment.

It helps to know that our tendencies toward distraction will use every device in the book to seduce us, trick us, cajole or threaten us into abandoning the fulfilling experience of Being, just so we will continue to experience the old distractions that are so familiar to us.

We eventually tire of the apparently endless cycles of desiring things, working to obtain them, only to become disillusioned, disappointed or even disgusted upon finally having them. We keep trying to still the next desire, repeating the cycle until we are firmly embedded in a rut.

Our cravings increase in direct proportion
to our distractions.

Hence the old adage, "The more you have, the more you need." Objects tend to entangle us in ever-increasing cycles of mechanical complexities, rather than relieving our needs and anxieties.

It is through meditation that you attain relief from such nonsensical compulsions. In meditation, you find such deep enrichment in the clear experience of your essential Being, such real, lasting and totally dependable substance, that the ephemeral nature of the distractions is exposed. They lose their power to seduce and compel you against your better judgment. In meditation you savor each moment in conscious, peaceful, rich existence.

CHAPTER TWENTY-THREE

MEDITATION IS LIVING LIFE WELL

"If something is worth doing, it is worth doing well." This is a popular saying in our society. It certainly applies to your life.

If life is worth living,
it is worth living well.

By the very fact that you are going on with your life you attest to the basic tenet that it is worth living. Then you might as well participate in it consciously—that is to say, so you know it is happening—and enjoy life fully. That is living well.

Living well means
experiencing life spontaneously
from moment to moment
in continuity, in reality and at will.
That is meditation.

Living in meditation means taking charge of your life and claiming your life as the precious gift it is.

Nearly half our waking life is spent working. Many people sacrifice innumerable hours doing work they consider worthless to their lives except for the paycheck it yields. That is one of the great human tragedies. To protect your life from such tragedy, you can train yourself to relate all actions to your conscious experience of Being.

> *Each action,*
> *no matter how menial or mundane,*
> *can be seen as a way of experiencing*
> *the Being that you are.*

This awareness can free you from both attachment and repulsion. You will steadily expand and enhance the ability to express your Being, independent of conditions.

No work is seen as worthless or boring then. It becomes clear it is not the type of work that determines your experience, but how you relate to it.

> *A "worthwhile" action*
> *related to without consciousness*
> *turns worthless,*
> *while a "worthless" action*
> *related to with real consciousness*
> *turns worthwhile.*

When you act in consciousness, you act in relation to all forms of Being, in the awareness of what you really are: self-knowing interconnected Being. Thus your actions, in expressing that consciousness, are true to the wholeness to which you are integral.

This manner of action, conscious action that is true self-expression and experience, is born of meditation. Only in consciously enacting the Being that you are can you feel right about yourself and deeply at peace.

Because we live with so much tension and pressure, worry and hurry, there is much anxiety, depression and addiction. Bodies and minds are breaking down due to the corrosive effects of these stressors.

It is all so unnecessary. You do not have to permit these unconscious stress-inducing ways of living to dictate your experience.

In meditation you can experience the beautiful power of calm and steady faculties responding effectively to your subtlest directions. Then you are not subject to the distractive caprices of weak and undisciplined faculties. Instead you feel secure and confident in your own quiet strength.

As you can gaze through the unruffled waters
to the very depths
of the tranquil mountain lake,
so can you during meditation
see deeply within your very Being.

During meditation, you let go of the incessant involvement with the problems of work, relationships and passing events. You stop your worries and schemes. You detach yourself from the compulsive slavery to circumstances and conditions that tend to take life over.

In meditation all turbulence settles down,
the inner muddy waters clear up,
and the vision of the wholeness of Being
pulls together.

Your mind and all your faculties become one integral instrument finely attuned, powerfully focused and wonderfully skilled and capable. In this unobstructed view of yourself and your life, the most advantageous direction for you to take becomes self-evident.

You will see clearly what you really want and how to most effectively direct your actions toward attaining it. In the state of meditation you experience that you are innately much stronger than you previously knew.

In the human state you appear as a distinct energy pattern within the limitless field of energy that is the infinite Being.

As the eddy is integral to the stream,
so are you integral
to the limitless Power of Being.

The various energy patterns composing your mental, psychological and physical aspects make up your individual force-field. Within this limited perspective, the energy patterns are potentially subject to external and internal energy drains.

Contemporary research has shown that our force-field is strengthened and maintained in direct proportion to the strength of meditation. With meditation, brain waves become stronger and less erratic, more even, depicting a deeper level of functioning. The neurological system is then subtly balanced and acutely attuned while free of tension.

Hypertension releases its stranglehold upon the nervous system, thereby removing constriction from the cardiovascular system. This results in enormous relief for the heart.

In meditation you consciously dwell in the simple and direct moment of being. You experience all your resources in harmonious integration and live spontaneously, skillfully and zestfully, at will, with balanced joy.

CHAPTER TWENTY-FOUR

THE ACT OF
OVERCOMING LIMITATIONS

Meditation is the experience of total Being. The Being that we are fundamentally is not an object but an energy, a power. We are fundamentally the power by which everything about us exists, the Power of Being. That is our real identity. Power is limitless, all-pervasive in time and space.

Dwelling in
the clear and unhindered experience
of your real identity,
the limitless Power of Being,
is meditation.

In order to consider the state of meditation meaningfully, completely clear your mind right now, so it is like a fresh field upon which you can experience the deep knowledge that resides within.

169

Clear your mind of all preconceptions, questions and quarrels, of fancy schemes and brilliant ideas. For these moments allow your mind to be still—absorbed in the inner quietude.

For most of us, it is rare to experience the grand scope of total Being. Yet that wholeness is what we really are and what our life is all about.

In order to be fulfilled,
to be at peace,
you require the unlimited experience
of the wholeness of Being that you are.

We find ourselves in a world where we are constantly engaged in activity. Ultimately, our actions have our satisfaction and fulfillment as their sole purpose. However, we meet on our path many limitations that repeatedly frustrate us to the point of making it impossible to find peace. There is an ill-defined but gnawing feeling that something is missing in our lives, or even within us.

We may attempt to fill the inner emptiness by a variety of objects or activities, by changes of circumstance, time or place. We may aim with great ambition to become successful at our job, or seek fulfillment in relationships or through religious involvement. We may try any of these or even all of these and still find frustration.

There is a feeling behind it all that something is missing, or incomplete, limited. It may seem that we will find limitations wherever we search, in whatever we try.

Meditation is the full experience
of the limitless Being that you are.
Thus it follows that meditation
is the act of overcoming all limitations.

Here is where our little minds perk up to say, 'But I'm only human. How can I overcome my limitations?' It is pertinent to remember that as 'only human' you are highly advanced on the evolutionary ladder.

Evolution is the continuous process
of development toward a state
free of limitation.

Is such a state possible? Of course it is.

Nature would not be so perverse
as to direct all its forces
toward a goal that is not attainable.

But is this evolutionary goal of freedom from limitation possible for us humans? If it were not possible for such highly placed beings on the evolutionary ladder, human beings, then of whom could it be expected? Why do we possess such amazingly powerful and skilled faculties, just to stay the same?

The Power of Being manifests itself through all life forms. Evolution is the process by which the manifestations of Being grow toward recognition of themselves as the Being they really are.

When you see yourself clearly
in relationship to the thrust of evolution,
your limitations are recognized
as products of your mistaken ideas
regarding your identity,
which, after all, is limitless Being.
From the evolutionary perspective,
the human potential to transcend limitations
is recognized as imminent actuality.

The habitual opposition to that view lies in the tendency to allow ourselves to be manipulated into a state of ever-deepening self-limitation. We buy the bill of goods that says we are miserable sinners born into a vale of sorrows. What that implies about the creative force behind such a scheme, is too disrespectful to contemplate.

Your own innermost urges and drives, your ultimate inspirations and ambitions, give you ample evidence of the evolutionary force that is at the core of all your motivations. That force will not cease in you until you have completely answered it by realizing your potential and ultimate fulfillment.

For many years of your life you may have attempted to answer the inner urge toward fulfillment by filling your moments with superficial sensations. They fill you with nothing but disappointment, which is then followed by frustration and, eventually, despair.

You know from repeated personal experience that no matter how great or numerous the objects of partial pleasure attained, you are always driven to press further. You will not find real satisfaction until you have reached the limitless, the ultimate.

Meditation is the act of overcoming all imagined limitations, and of merging with the infinite fulfillment.

When you evolve to the pinnacle experience
of your essential Being,
which is of the nature of limitlessness,
the evolutionary process is fulfilled in you.

Then you actually experience the indescribable fulfillment toward which everything throughout nature is continuously compelled.

Meditation is the genuine experience
of human being fulfilled.

CHAPTER TWENTY-FIVE

THE ROUSING OF THE SOUL

Meditation is the rousing of the innermost essence, what we call our spirit or soul. During meditation the essential force is experienced in self-recognition and self-expression.

This is rare in most lives, as our attention is usually absorbed by the activities of senses and mind; they demand exclusivity. The performance of one function necessitates ignoring, suppressing or diminishing others. This results in fragmented experience as opposed to the continuity and wholeness that you experience during meditation.

Meditation is self-experience
in full consciousness.

Your life experienced during those calm, clear moments involves the totality of your Being. When your soul comes thus to the fore, you are deeply enriched by the moment. You enjoy a depth of incomparable satisfaction, a flood of total Being that answers the soul's need for self-expression. You may remember glimpses of such spontaneous experiences from childhood.

175

During meditation you experience the power of your spirit as irresistible, for the soul is the essence of the entire Being; it is not a partial aspect of the personality that can be ignored or suppressed with impunity for the sake of other insistent needs.

Your soul is the all-inclusive,
all-unifying essence
of your entire Being.

To neglect or suppress your essence is to stifle the experience of your very Being. That guarantees frustration and failure. When you allow the power of your essence to shine forth in meditation, it gives rise to an experience of magnificent clarity and understanding and joy. There is then no fragmentation by exclusivity, externality, partiality or any other limitation; you experience the wholeness of Being.

The essential force,
the Being that in essence you are,
rising into self-experiencing expression,
is meditation.

Though this is our most natural, direct and simple mode of being, we seldom are in that state. Our lives are often so confused and distracted by false conception and illusion, that we lose sight of who and why we are, and completely forgo experiencing the clarity and fullness of our Being.

No wonder people spend millions of dollars annually hiring experts to dissolve their identity crisis, the contemporary malaise. No one can do it for you, though. You alone can martial the forces which remove the old hindrances standing in the way of the simple and natural experience of the Being that you are. Meditation is that experience.

It is important to remember that in meditation you are not grasping for something outside yourself. You are unveiling the wealth within.

Remember always that in essence
you are the Power of Being.
That is your identity.

The ramifications of that realization are vast. In reality, there is no limit to your potential, for we know power to be illimitable. This is not to be confused with the body. We know that the body's potential is limited. But you are not this body. Your body is not your identity; it is but one of the means by which your identity, the Power of Being, is experienced and expressed. You are the essential force that empowers your body and all your faculties.

The Being that you are
is here simply to
experience and express
Self in reality.

Such self-experience and self-expression yield lasting satisfaction. You can derive real satisfaction only from being true to the meaning of your Being.

When we are not accustomed to being in that steady state of clear experience, meditation can seem so vague and difficult. But remember, the difficulty lies in a life that is lived devoid of its real meaning, not in meditation.

Once you recognize the fundamental necessity of relating your life experience to your actual identity, you can learn a series of effective techniques to guide yourself, step-by-step in ascending order, through experiences of deeper and wider meditation. A real teacher, one who speaks of and works from direct experience and intimate knowledge of that cherished state, will provide invaluable aid.

DECISIONS FOR
LASTING SUCCESS

CHAPTER TWENTY-SIX

FIVE FUNDAMENTAL CONSIDERATIONS FOR SUCCESSFUL DECISION-MAKING

Would you not agree that in our society we are busily engaged in action during much of our waking time? For what purpose?

You engage in action to improve your life. No matter how much improvement you accomplish, however, you cannot rest until you have achieved your ultimate aim: fulfillment.

Fulfillment is only possible if your actions are in agreement with what really would fulfill you. And here lies the rub. Although we keep busy in the pursuit of the pleasures and satisfactions, as well as the circumstances and conditions that we hope will bring us fulfillment, our actions, when closely examined, can be seen to frequently contradict the fulfillment we seek.

Observe someone else sometime and see how that person approaches an action; see if the approach allows for success. Then observe yourself with the same detachment.

Often we set out to achieve something and become frustrated by the failure set up by our own actions. Usually this is due to a failure in the decision-making process leading up to our actions.

For your actions to turn out successfully, five fundamental considerations are indispensable:

1. Decide what you really want.

2. Determine what is required of you to achieve what you really want.

3. Decide what is more important to you: what you really want or what opposes it within you.

4. Make a clear determination that you will do what is needed to achieve what you really want.

5. Align your faculties and your actions with the desired goal.

Reading these points you might think, 'Of course, that only makes sense.' But it can happen all too often that we fail to include points of simple awareness in our approach to an action, and then suffer failure. So let us look at these fundamentals in more detail.

DECIDING WHAT YOU REALLY WANT

You know how a dog who has trouble deciding where he wants to lie down can circle around and around before finally settling in? Recently I saw a man in the supermarket acting like that. He had come there because he knew he wanted something, but he surely did not know exactly what he wanted.

I decided to watch him as he ambled about aimlessly placing items into his shopping cart, returning them soon after—often to the wrong shelf—wasting his energy and looking quite dissatisfied with himself, in fact frustrated. And the collection of foods he ended up with at the cash register! If he had made up his mind beforehand and made a list, he would have been much more successful.

Sometimes you may feel too lazy to make the mental effort to decide what you want before you go into action. As a consequence you have to spend much more effort to make up for that initial laziness. Now, the example regarding grocery shopping is relatively small. The need to decide what you want becomes infinitely greater when you consider your life. Since all your actions have your fulfillment as their purpose, it is a fundamental necessity for you to come to a clear understanding of what you really want before you act.

Your ultimate purpose, therefore your deepest want, is to experience in full consciousness the wholeness of Being; that is the only way for you to be fulfilled. You know you cannot rest until you dwell in that state. All the transient pleasures yield to disappointment and frustration.

We have a tendency to favor the temporary at the expense of the lasting; we go for the quick fix. The temporary binds, the lasting liberates.

As long as we are bound up in the pattern of grasping for the momentary, we will be too preoccupied to avail ourselves of the permanent. We will be bound to cycles of wanting and attaining that yield to disappointment.

Those cycles grow into frustration that lasts until another passing fancy catches us up again. To liberate yourself from such vicious cycles you have to keep in mind what you really want, what really fulfills you.

Since your ultimate fulfillment lies in the experience and expression of the Power of Being that you are, you can ask yourself:

Will this course of action
reveal the experience of Being
or
conceal the experience of Being?

With this you have a yardstick which invariably serves you in making the choices by which you direct your life to fulfillment.

DETERMINING WHAT IS REQUIRED OF YOU TO ACHIEVE WHAT YOU REALLY WANT

Sometimes we rush into action, aiming at a goal without giving a thought to what it takes to attain that particular goal. This frequently results in our quitting the action before achieving success. Consequently we may be disappointed or even disgusted with ourselves.

Most things in life have a price, be it money, time, energy or other resources. We would not think of buying a car or a house, for example, without first finding out what it costs.

When it comes to dedicating our actions to a goal, we would do well to first assess what we need to devote to its achievement. This assessment may reveal to us that we do not really want or need that particular attainment. Thus we can quit the idea before investing any action in it.

On the other hand, our assessment may make it even clearer to us that we do want to attain the particular goal. In that case, clear assessment will motivate us to begin the actions which focus our forces most directly toward the achievement of our goal.

Deciding What Is More Important To You

One of the prevalent themes I have noticed in my psychological and spiritual guidance of students, is a fierce attachment to the behaviors that oppose their goals.

When, for example, Arnold wanted to add a room to his house, he complained that it could take years, cost tens of thousands of dollars and be extremely complicated. Arnold's attachment to the negative was such that he spent his energy and ingenuity thinking up as many obstacles as possible. The same dynamics tend to come even more powerfully into play when it comes to making changes within ourselves.

Some individuals can become
impressively creative in enumerating
even the most remotely conceivable obstacles
to what they really want.

A simple principle involved in our negativity regarding action is inertia. Inertia opposes change; it would have things remain as they are.

For you to initiate an action that changes the status quo, you have to overcome the force of inertia. You do that by purposefully applying a force which opposes inertia.

Arnold, wanting to add to his house, for example, could free himself from the clutches of inertia by first coming up with as many ideas as possible without worrying about their practicality. He would thereby build such a strong current of positivity that the negativity would have little chance to arise. In that positive state he would find it relatively easy to select from the numerous ideas and form a realistic strategy toward attainment of his goal.

*If you want to bring about
the life you really want,
you have to overcome inertia
by countering it
with positive force,
with ways of thinking, feeling and acting
in the direction of your choice.*

Another person comes to mind, Jeanette, who felt stuck in a static state. Jeanette habitually thought negatively about herself. She suffered severe difficulties when she considered acting on any of her needs or desires.

Jeanette attempted to justify her inertia by rationalizing that she was not worth the effort anyway. This was in direct opposition to plentiful evidence to the contrary. Jeanette was frequently praised for her obvious goodness, intelligence and beauty.

Having been frozen for so long in inactivity, Jeanette's pain became unbearable. Only then did she rouse the energy within to seek help: help in learning to overcome the fear of change that had been induced by her inertia. She decided she definitely preferred changing the way she related to herself, over maintaining her inactive state. Thus Jeanette was ready for the next step in successful decision-making.

MAKING A CLEAR DETERMINATION TO DO WHAT IS NEEDED TO ACHIEVE WHAT YOU REALLY WANT

By this time in the process, enough positive force has been built up that it is easy to initiate action in the direction of your real goal. You have decided what you really want, and you have made up your mind that you will place your focus on the attainment of your goal rather than on what could possibly stand in your way. You determine, in full integrity and trust in yourself, to take action.

ALIGNING YOUR FACULTIES AND YOUR ACTIONS WITH THE GOAL

Now is the time to really go for it. You throw your full resources, your body and mind, your feelings, emotions and senses, intellect and intuition, unhesitatingly into the activities that will bring you the results you want. Jeanette eventually learned a lesson of critical importance:

> *Rather than waste your energy*
> *proving to yourself*
> *how you cannot make things work,*
> *apply your energy to proving*
> *how you can.*

This directness of approach allows you to attain your goals with relative effortlessness and grace, because you eliminate the struggle against the resistance put up by inertia and by the fear of change.

> *Many people make the mistake*
> *of initiating their actions hesitantly,*
> *thereby encouraging the resistances.*

This can result in drawn-out struggles at great expense of energy, time and—especially—self-confidence. The easier and more successful approach is to do what you set out to do. You affirm your integrity and trustworthiness by engaging directly in the actions that allow you to effectively attain what you really want in life.

The five fundamental considerations for successful decision-making help you flourish as an Expert In Life.™

CHAPTER TWENTY-SEVEN

CONSCIOUSLY CHOOSING ACTIONS
THAT YIELD BENEFICIAL RESULTS

There are but two types of actions: those yielding momentary—or imagined—pleasure, and those yielding lasting—or real—fulfillment. The former lead to bondage, the latter to liberation. The choice is yours.

If the decision is to live willy-nilly according to every passing fancy, then you just struggle from moment to moment in constant reaction to the shifting and changing circumstances and conditions. That will be your fate until you decide to claim the conscious experience of your Being.

If you do not want to doom yourself to a fate of bondage to the ephemeral, you have to make a decision to direct your actions and life in accord with what gives you lasting satisfaction. There are times in our life when we experience the deepest urge and the highest aspiration to direct our life to the fulfillment of our potential. You owe it to yourself to respond to these strong impulses with direct action.

If we are not in the habit of enacting our life expertly and directly, it behooves us to begin doing so by the purposeful performance of positive actions.

> *Positive practice is guaranteed to yield*
> *powerful, beneficial effects*
> *when you devote yourself to it*
> *with sincerity,*
> *in continuity,*
> *with trust in yourself*
> *and with expert means.*

WITH SINCERITY

When you respond to your inspiration by making a true and powerful decision to henceforth live to the best of your ability in accord with your potential, you have made a quantum step in your evolution. You do not pay lip service to such a decision; you make it from the clear motivation of your intelligent free will. This also means you will not allow yourself to fall into the self-deception of telling yourself that you are doing what you ought to be doing, while not really doing it at all. There is no "ought to" about it—only free, knowing choice.

From the moment you make a true decision to engage in positive practice, your life is irrevocably dedicated to its purpose. Your actions are consistently related to your real fulfillment.

IN CONTINUITY

Dedicating your life to the positive practice of behaviors and actions that fulfill your inspirations is not to be regarded as a burden. Rather, it removes the overwhelming energy drain of the negative effects you would suffer as a result of actions contrary to your fulfillment.

Your sincere decision to direct life
toward lasting fulfillment
becomes the standard
by which you measure
all actions
and future decisions.

Although the decision to direct life to fulfillment has meaning only if you are determined to honor it in continuity, to honor it by actually practicing the positive ways of life, it soon becomes clear that it is not a matter of length of time. The fundamental meaning of Being is permanent and unchanging, as must be your committed relationship to it, your positive living of it.

If you were invited to step out of the desert of deprivation and sorrow into a kingdom of fulfillment and joy, would you worry, 'For how long?' We do not worry about how long we should breathe, nor do we make faint passes at breathing now and then. Similarly, let us not make momentary passes at directing our life toward fulfillment.

The process and experience of life,
and life itself,
are one.

Involved in life devoted to fulfillment, you are so fascinated and absorbed in the spontaneous and unadulterated experience of each moment, that you have neither the inclination nor the time to wonder or worry how long fulfillment will take.

WITH TRUST IN YOURSELF

An inevitable result of devoting your life to the fulfillment of who you really are is the development of trust in your Being.

You recognize
that your Being is ultimately worthy,
worthy of being consciously addressed
with each life experience and action.

WITH EXPERT MEANS

To transform your thoughts and inspirations into action is important, yet not enough. The proper means are required: right action. Right action is based upon self-knowledge and relates your actions expertly to who you really are.

Expertise in action is highly advantageous to you. By consciously cultivating behaviors and actions that yield positive results, you are congruent to yourself and thereby fulfilled.

You deserve to have a life sincerely, continuously and expertly devoted—with trust in the Being that you are—to the fulfillment of your potential.

CHAPTER TWENTY-EIGHT

Strengthening Your Faculties Through Positive Practice

It is easy for us to agree that we want to lead a life in which we fulfill our potential. We want to experience ourselves in wholeness and truth.

From our own experiences we know, however, that there are factors within and about us which oppose such a meaningful life experience. If we are honest with ourselves, we acknowledge that we have become thoroughly habituated and attached to our long-standing patterns of self-opposition.

At times we may be aware that we could live more effectively and gain real satisfaction. However, our faculties—our body and mind, our emotions, feelings and senses, our intellect and intuition—often are engaged in behaviors that result in our disappointment and frustration.

We have the unique good fortune
to be in possession
of an amazing array of faculties
that empower us to experience our real Being
on every possible level.

When we find our faculties occupied with dysfunctional behaviors, we can become quite alarmed and even discouraged to the point of depression. As adults, we suffer shame and guilt as a consequence.

We are quite unconcerned when we see an infant's mind lacking in power and skill, for we know that this little mind will grow with proper use into a marvelous instrument. In adulthood, all the human faculties can be developed to their full capacity.

You know and experience yourself
and the world you live in
according to the degree
that you have trained your faculties
to function in service
to the Being you really are.

Unfortunately, for the overwhelming majority of us, our training is severely limited to a rather unbalanced and lackadaisical approach. Sure, we play some games and sports to strengthen the body, and we spend many years in school to develop our mind.

However, what systematic practice have we engaged in to develop our other faculties, such as our emotions, feelings and intuition? What have we done to develop a sense of moral judgment and ethical discrimination? Do we not recognize the advantage, indeed the necessity of such development that allows us to lead our lives as balanced, evolving and self-empowered human beings?

The concept of gathering all our faculties into harmonious and effective unity, as well as nurturing and strengthening them, seems strange to us. We need to learn to establish ourselves in those positive patterns.

Do you consider the unified wholeness of your faculties insignificant to your life? Do you want to just leave its development subject to chance? Most of us would answer with a resounding, "No!"

A common saying is, "Use it, or lose it." Conversely, if you use a faculty repeatedly in the proper way, you gain it; you gain the faculty in the sense of having its functions serve you. This can transform that faculty into a powerfully effective instrument capable of helping you toward real success and satisfaction.

Through being effectively utilized, your faculties grow in the ability to perform their intended function. Repeated and intelligent application of your faculties in service to the Being you really are, is positive practice.

> *Positive practice is*
> *sincere and continuous repetition*
> *of chosen beneficial behaviors,*
> *without backsliding,*
> *based on expert means,*
> *with trust in the Being*
> *that you really are.*

It is through positive practice that we free ourselves from the tyranny of our own negative habits. Negative habits bind us to self-limiting and self-destructive patterns of life.

The purpose of practice is to make our aspirations come true. You may have the aspiration to be a good tennis player, but you know very well that only through plenty of proper practice can you expect to become really good at the game. You might aspire to the easy familiarity with a musical instrument that will permit you the pleasure of self-expression through music. Practice is certainly required. To achieve proficiency in the faculties through which you lead your life—be they physical or mental, emotional, psychological or intellectual—you engage in positive practice.

Positive practice
is the purposeful repetition of chosen actions
to achieve expertise.

Clearly, our life and our fulfillment are important enough for us to make it a high priority to become expert at conducting our life. This life expertise does not come to us by default, wishful thinking or passive waiting. Rather, we become Expert In Life™ proactively by systematically pursuing it.

You become a student of life. The Expert In Life system places at your disposal direct experiences, profound knowledge and many powerful techniques that can help you become significantly more skillful and well-rounded in leading your life.

The mere study through books of how to achieve real fulfillment is not enough. The positive potential of your learning will only affect your life when you take your studies out of the realm of theory and apply them in actuality.

As an Expert In Life you consistently act in accord with the expanded perspective you gain through your steadily deepening experience of reality. You change not only how you look at your life, but also how you enact your life. You change your behaviors, your ways of being.

The steady application of your learning
through practice
provides life experience.
In applying the knowledge
gained by experience
continuously
to your behaviors and actions,
you cultivate wisdom.

By means of positive practice you learn to empower and direct the faculties through which you perceive and enact life. This allows you to lead your life toward infinitely greater satisfaction.

You experience yourself clearly, express yourself effectively and become strong, vital and accomplished on every level. Through the positive practice of behaviors that express who you really are, you claim and exert your birthright of free will and become joyously self-determining.

THE JOY OF COMMITMENT

CHAPTER TWENTY-NINE

RESPONDING TO LIFE

There are times when we feel ourselves uplifted by an enthusiastic energy arising from deep within us. It is an innate force that wants to respond to life wholeheartedly and spontaneously. However, when this energy arises, it is sometimes countered by a tendency in us to stop as if dead in our tracks. What accounts for such inhibiting tendencies?

We may fear that we are not good enough, not deserving. We may even attempt to seek false comfort in the familiar misery caused by the patterns of hope and disappointment—the games we perpetrate upon ourselves, the fantasies, the lies.

Sometimes we carefully maintain the attitude, 'If only such and such missing ingredients were to be added to my life, then I could be happy'—as if that gave us an excuse to not respond to life as it is.

> *Were we to attain what we say we want,*
> *we would have to come out from hiding*
> *behind the wall of excuses*
> *and live life as it is,*
> *spontaneously and joyously.*

That is where the coward in us draws the line. When we meet the opportunity to have what we have been yearning for, we evade it. Here we have the ultimate example of the fear of success leading to irresponsibility—the refusal to apply our ability to respond to life.

So then we respond to fear, not to life's urgings; we honor the imaginary, not the real; life is deferred, not lived now. We turn away from what is truly dear to us and fall for false promises of passing pleasures.

And we struggle. We try fooling ourselves with partial commitments that of course, really lead nowhere and are no commitments at all. We suffer the agonizing frustration of feeling stuck in limbo between the predictable hollowness of the life we are attached to and the challenge of what we innately need. Limbo is painful to bear.

The self-denial and destruction
caused by cowardice
shame the soul.
As long as we are unwilling
to commit ourselves to positive action,
we remain bound to negative tendencies.

The situation cannot be borne indefinitely. So we strike out in anger, not against self-delusions, but against the real fulfillment that beckons to us. We behave as if we could eliminate our fear and indecision by destroying any possibility of our own fulfillment.

Thus it is not uncommon for a person in such emotional turmoil to react with denial or even outright aggression toward someone whose very love and concern could be of positive aid. Helpful methods are discredited. Thus, people who embrace commitment become grave irritants to those who avoid it.

It makes no sense at all
for us to shirk responsibility,
since by doing so we discard
our very ability to respond to life.

Dependence upon drugs or alcohol, for example, has dulled in countless people their ability to consciously participate in life. So it is for excessive television watching, overeating and overworking. Neither those nor any other ways of avoiding our response to life—compulsive worrying, fantasizing, rationalizing—have ever made anyone really happy.

Just as a mistaken relationship to responsibility cuts down our potential to enjoy life, so does an erroneous relationship to commitment assure our failure. We cannot succeed at any-thing—be it our work, relationships, meditation or life itself—unless we respond to it as it is and commit ourselves to conduct that is harmonious with our goal.

Deep within us resides the immutable voice of truth. No matter how tricky our self-deceptions, somehow we always know there is not a smoke-screen thick enough to consistently conceal our goal from us.

> *The challenge of a truly successful life*
> *is not only to discern what you really want,*
> *but to respond to that intrinsic longing*
> *by committing yourself to fulfilling it.*

This is the logical next step. After all, there is no sense in doing anything else—anything that does not bring you closer to fulfillment.

You end any involvement with vague wishing and delusive waiting and enthusiastically engage in a course of action that favors fulfillment. You spurn the superficial involvements that always end up disappointing you, leaving you aching for more and more. You stop merely testing the waters with your toes and plunge into the ocean of life with joyous commitment.

CHAPTER THIRTY

RESPONSIBILITY
THE ANSWER TO LIFE'S CALL

THE CALL AND THE ANSWER

> *The joy of your aspirations*
> *arises within you*
> *when you respond to them;*
> *the agony of your life*
> *descends upon you*
> *when you let them die.*

Once we have decided what we really want, and have noted the obstacles—our failure patterns, fears and illusions—how can we proceed toward the success to which our life aspires?

We need to honor the fact that we are capable of responding to life's conditions. It is our responsibility to convert life's challenges into our successes. This responsibility is to be fulfilled by engaging, without attachment, the full force of our will in applying the proper means—with sincerity, faith, enthusiasm and persistence.

That is the answer to our innate yearnings and drives that are calling for fulfillment. It is an important answer. Let us look at it in detail.

The process of life is a persistent opening of ourselves to ever subtler understanding and enjoyment of all levels and facets of existence. Each part of our Being demands to be known and expressed until we feel complete in the experience of its fullness. Our aspirations goad us and guide us toward that fulfillment. This is the call of life, and it demands to be answered.

Life declares itself exuberantly all around us by simply saying, "I am." This "I am" is affirmed by our Being, too, but there is also that part in us that wants to declare itself in response.

As human beings, we have the unique privilege and opportunity to respond inwardly—with spiritual initiative—to the call of life. We need to acknowledge and remember that.

> *Life expresses itself in innumerable ways,*
> *but no matter what the time or circumstance,*
> *there is always within you*
> *the ability to respond.*

Knowing this can give you the confidence and energy to meet life's challenges not only bravely, but also with a sense of joy.

The ability to respond is what we call responsibility. Many of us have an ambivalent relationship to responsibility. One would think that every human being would just love this wonderful gift: to be able to respond to life with all its changes and challenges that are its colors and textures. These are life's expressions; they empower us to feel life, to see it, to experience it—to respond to it. How wonderful that we are able to respond! What would life be for us without that responsibility?

Yet we often shun responsibility. We habitually consider it a burden; we are afraid of it. What kind of person do you admire, though: one who shuns responsibility, or one who assumes responsibility? Most of us would agree on the latter.

We consider a responsible person attractive, desirable: the ideal. The inner strength of such a person stimulates us. Although we are drawn to a responsible person, we tend to shy away from the opportunity to exercise responsibility in our own life.

Some of us try to take on other people's responsibilities while avoiding our own. The self-sacrificing provider of the family who neglects himself, or the "devoted" wife who tries to live for her husband and to forget herself, are examples of unrealistic and destructive relationships to responsibility.

You can see how a false conception of responsibility breeds an ambivalent relationship to it. Your ability to respond to life is an integral part of your Being. Without it there can be no joyous experience of the very fact that you exist. Ambivalence toward such an essential aspect of life causes painful conflicts.

Life invites you to respond to it fully.

It is our misconception of responsibility that causes problems when we are faced with life's invitation. Instead of enjoying our ability to respond to life's rich opportunities, we shrink back toward inaction, lifelessness, fear.

The opportunity to answer life then becomes perverted into a fear of death. No wonder we meet the fear of death; when we turn our back on our ability to respond to life, we inevitably are turned toward its opposite, death.

Turning away from responsibility
is the cause of our turmoil,
not responsibility itself.

We can never find refuge in irresponsibility. There is absolutely no advantage in obscuring our response to life by fantasizing, rationalizing or in any other way evading it. That only brings problems. These problems will grow into crises, and we know from experience that crisis forces us to face reality almost always in painful ways.

Responding to reality only after having been forced into it by the pressure of crisis is irresponsible in itself. We are acting then as if an outer force could take over and make our decisions for us. Then we have to answer its demands, not the urgings of our own free will. That is a rather gross game of self-deception and destruction. It never works.

You cannot fulfill life
by refusing to respond to it.

Once we recognize our innate ability to truly respond to life, we must not contradict it. To do so is to violate ourselves in the most destructive manner.

Life demands to be experienced and expressed, not shunned and suppressed. False conceptions and distortions of our Being will not answer that demand; only our real Being will.

The drive to lead your life
consciously and responsively
will be neither deterred
nor suppressed;
and that is your saving grace.
We all are gifted
with the ability to respond
to the full force of our Being.

*Life calls upon you
to own up to this ability,
to be intimately aware of it,
to accept life,
and thereby yourself,
in reality.*

HOW TO ENJOY RESPONSIBILITY

Our misconceptions regarding responsibility have to be eliminated. How? By clearing away the muddle of falsity with the clarity of truth.

When we see ourselves relating irresponsibly to life, we can remind ourselves that this is part of old patterns rooted in misconceptions regarding ourselves and regarding responsibility. Then we can retrain ourselves through right thinking.

We need to assess what we really are and want, and then act upon it, respond to it! We need to act consistently and use self-discipline to overcome conditioning that stimulates a false relationship to our life.

Once you sincerely follow through with the knowledge that responsibility is a gift, you feel better, stronger, more positive. You move toward fulfillment by means of purposeful behavior. In your correct relation to responsibility, you are responding to what is called for within you.

*Responding to the inner call
yields fulfillment;
refusing to respond
yields frustration.*

Thus you learn by your experience that fulfillment is gained by your proper choices and responses. Clearly, responsibility is to be neither feared nor experienced as a burden; rather, it offers you the opportunity to appreciate your ability to be.

Recognizing this, you welcome responsibility at every opportunity, and embrace it with full consent. It is your beloved friend, not an enemy to be feared.

> *In responsibility*
> *you find life's refuge;*
> *in irresponsibility*
> *you turn toward death.*
> *Responsibility relates you to joy;*
> *irresponsibility to anxiety.*
> *Responsibility is the means*
> *of fully experiencing Being.*

LIFE IS RESPONSIBILITY

Life is a continuous opportunity to respond willingly and openly; to experience life fully is what we are all about. Ask yourself, 'Do I want to be limited to responding only on superficial levels, only on the grossest? Or do I want to respond to life fully and thereby experience myself with every aspect of my Being on the subtlest levels?'

> *If you want to enjoy*
> *the privilege and opportunity*
> *of experiencing life to the fullest,*
> *you have to respond to life as it is,*
> *not as you would like it to be,*
> *nor as you would design it to be,*
> *nor as you fear it to be,*
> *but as it is.*

You have the ability to live life fully, but can only do so by exercising your ability to respond, your responsibility. Wishing for the fulfilling experience of life will not do: you have to answer joyously to life. That is being truly responsive to yourself, with limitless acceptance. That is to truly love yourself: responsibility in the ultimate.

CHAPTER THIRTY-ONE

PROCRASTINATION
WHY TORTURE YOURSELF?

Procrastination is
the act of indefinitely delaying
the fulfillment of our intentions.

Procrastination is a painful and disempowering process to those of us who are enmeshed in it. Through procrastination we deprive ourselves of the powers inherent in our inspirations.

For example, when you receive a pure idea of something that you wish to do and that would benefit you to fulfill, you can, through your imagination, already experience the value and satisfaction you could gain. However:

Procrastination stops your positivity
by delaying the transformation
of inspiration into action.

Rather than giving us the satisfaction of having responded to our inspiration, procrastination gives us indecision and irresolution. We squirm with irritation, guilt and self-incrimination.

Why would we repeatedly torture ourselves in such frustrating ways? It is important to understand the dynamics that are behind procrastination.

NEGATIVE THINKING

The underlying cause of procrastination
is a false idea regarding ourselves.

Most of us subconsciously think of ourselves as far more limited and isolated than we really are. Therefore we automatically consider ourselves weak and incapable of the kinds of actions we would want to perform.

This negative way of thinking causes us to feel deeply insecure and distrusting of ourselves. Because of that, ironically, we demand that the functions we perform adhere to a standard of perfection which is beyond anything reasonable to expect from any human being. The result is that we are frozen in a static state.

We find ourselves caught in a terrible dilemma. On one hand we are attracted by the vitalizing and motivating energy of inspiration; on the other hand we feel imprisoned by inertia.

In procrastination
our energy seems frozen
by the lack of trust
in ourselves
and our abilities.

As a result of this stand-off, we feel even worse about ourselves. Soon we do not want to experience anything about ourselves any more, especially those heavy, painful feelings. After all, we have suffered long enough from the slings and arrows of the self-blame and self-doubt that result from procrastination. So we stop feeling. The repression of feeling results in depression. This explains how depression often is the outcome of procrastination.

The negative self-reinforcing cycle that we then find ourselves in makes it difficult for friends and family to be with us. Often people feel compelled to tell us how easily we could fulfill our intentions. Of course we usually end up feeling even worse about ourselves, because we still feel unable to respond.

As a result of our apparent inability to act, not only our life, but the lives of those around us can be severely marred. The disharmony and frustration, the guilt and blame, as well as the general dysfunction within our family and work relationships, take a heavy toll.

THINKING IN TERMS OF WHO YOU REALLY ARE

Procrastination neither disappears by itself nor can someone else remove it for us. What can you do about this problem of procrastination? Recognize this:

We tend to procrastinate
working on overcoming procrastination.

If you believe in taking care of fundamentals first, insist that you act decisively and rationally as a person of strength and capability. This is difficult though, if you are not in contact with who and what we really are.

The root cause of our problems,
be they personal or societal,
is a false concept of our identity.

Most of us do not know who we really are. In our society we unfortunately treat the question of our real identity like a theoretical hobby. Therefore this fundamentally important and utterly practical question remains largely unanswered. When we discover our real identity, we find that we have infinitely greater abilities and powers than we normally acknowledge in ourselves.

Even if we have not yet realized who we essentially are, it is important for us to acknowledge that we are human beings who have the ability to discern what is favorable to us. We have the innate ability to decide what we intend, and to apply our will to performing those behaviors and actions that will fulfill our intentions to our satisfaction.

It is also important to recognize that, even when we are clear about what we want and how to attain it, the automatic mental patterns which insist that we are unable and weak may persist, in spite of much evidence to the contrary. We have to be persistent in acknowledging our fundamental human strengths and abilities of self-empowerment and self-determination.

When we look back at our personal history, we find that we eventually end up doing at least some of the things we want to do anyway. So we might as well be smart, as well as kinder to ourselves, by not first torturing ourselves with long periods of procrastination. We all know how painful they can be.

We can adopt the pose of an outside observer and say, 'Look, I have gone through this before. I have procrastinated until I felt so miserable that I eventually propelled myself into action and did what I intended. This proves that I have the ability. Why weaken myself first with torturous procrastination? I will go ahead now in full strength and do what I intend.'

Imagine for example, that you are looking ahead to the holidays and thinking, 'Well, I need to start planning how we, parents and children alike, are going to spend the holidays.' You start the process of making plans.

This is usually where the trouble begins. When something is still vague, it seems difficult to make it take shape.

Do not demand of yourself
to start with the finished plan.

Instead of planning for the whole season, start examining options, a few at a time. You can be more relaxed about it with a sense of unattachment and fluidity.

You might jot down any number of ideas and allow the flow of action to take place. An action as seemingly small as writing your ideas upon a piece of paper can begin the flow of actions leading to a wonderful result.

At the initial stage, do not think in terms of good or bad, effective or ineffective, expensive or inexpensive. Keep in mind the general principle of first letting the flow of action take place. Then you will find that one thing inspires the next; as we say, one thing leads to another. Then procrastination does not have a chance.

Eventually your "problem" becomes that you have too many ideas and plans, and you are in the enviable position of eliminating things, as opposed to being stuck in procrastination and not having started anything yet.

Taking Action

Keep reminding yourself
that it is pleasurable and satisfying
to engage in action
directed toward the fulfillment
of your intentions.

It is highly frustrating and dissatisfying to allow yourself to stay frozen in inaction due to an underlying distrust of your own strength and ability.

Remember,
the automatic negative thinking
regarding you, your abilities and strengths,
is fundamentally untrue.
It is a false pattern
that needs to be uprooted.

The most effective way by which you can uproot the false negative thinking is by proving it wrong. You prove it wrong not merely by positive affirmations, but by actions that bring home the point of the abilities and strengths that are inherent to you.

Procrastination is a torturous way of inflicting guilt and self-doubt upon ourselves.

You overcome procrastination
by purposefully engaging
in a flow of self-determined actions
that lead to your fulfillment.

I have found in my years of providing spiritual counseling that most of us have frequent hopes of changing the way we relate to ourselves. However, the hopes seem to be more frequent than the changes.

That is why we have created at The Nataraja Yoga Ashram a uniquely effective approach to making powerful positive change in our lives: the Expert In Life™ program. In this systematic approach, participants build a thorough foundation of self-understanding by means of their own direct experience. Replacing the negativity with which we normally view ourselves, they learn to instill within themselves a deep knowledge of their inherent strength.

Students base the transformation of their thinking regarding themselves not only on learning through teachings, but on real experience by which they truly know, not merely believe. They become experts at knowing the instruments through which they conduct their lives, and at empowering, fine-tuning and strengthening them.

Skilled in the use of your faculties, thus confident in yourself, you are freed from the energy drain of procrastination and flow forward with the energy of your inspiration toward the realization of your fondest dreams. You then discover your freedom and inherent ability to claim your life fulfillment.

CHAPTER THIRTY-TWO

THE COURAGE OF COMMITMENT

One hot summer day while swimming in the ocean, I saw a group of boys approaching the water. From their eager faces and enthusiastic comments it was clear that they were there to swim. Several boys ran straight into the water while others waded in more slowly. There soon was a general pandemonium of splashing, diving, laughing and frolicking.

I noticed that one of the boys had not yet joined his friends. As I casually observed him, he would test the water with his toes, take a few steps backward, then a few forward, and come to a halt, looking tentative and uncomfortable. After he had repeated this cycle several times, I heard him mutter that the water was not warm enough and that he did not really want to swim anyway. The boy stood alone, as if rooted to the spot, forlorn and miserable.

He watched the other boys as they were immersed in the water having a great time. This seemed to irritate him.

When his friends called him to join them, he shouted back that he was not really interested, the water was too cold. They replied that cold water was what they had wanted in order to cool off. He responded in a flush of anger that they were stupid, and retreated to a spot on the beach, isolated from everyone else, to soak in his misery.

It touched me how this boy's experience was similar to the plight suffered by so many people. If he had just dived in, he could have enjoyed himself; after all, that was what he wanted.

He had probably even anticipated the cooling comfort of the ocean while making his way through the hot day. Instead of proceeding with his plans, he was halted by hesitancy when it came to the moment of taking the plunge, of committing himself to the water. Instead of overcoming what could have been merely momentary hesitation, he succumbed to it and suffered miserably.

We spend so many moments wanting and waiting for the time of fulfillment to arrive. We know we shall not rest, cannot be at peace, until we are fulfilled. To gain fulfillment, we have to commit ourselves to it.

It helps us to remember to keep our focus on what we really want. We need to assess our condition, our weaknesses and strengths, and find the proper way to direct our life toward fulfillment. To involve ourselves with endeavors that do not bring us closer to fulfillment leads only to failure.

In our early attempts we may experience partial successes and failures as we stumble in response to our inner urgings toward the satisfaction of our needs. Experience teaches, and as we grow in self-understanding we advance in our ability to discern and to respond to our real needs. We learn important lessons, axioms to remember:

• *To disregard your innermost urgings is to neglect yourself.*
  —To respond to your innermost urgings
  is to honor yourself.

*• To follow every whim willy-nilly is to
court superficial pleasure, which not only derails you
from your self-determination but also fails to fulfill you.
—To follow a path true to yourself
is to be on the path to fulfillment.*

*• To forget life's lessons is to make experience meaningless.
—To integrate life's lessons
is to grow in the realization of your potential.*

Thus, your learning helps you become more clearly attuned to the subtler degrees of what you need for fulfillment. Gradually your ability to respond to those needs matures, and this guides you from the broad and ill-defined ways of juvenile fumblings onto a well-defined path that leads you ever more directly to your ultimate fulfillment.

Then you reach the crossroads of life, a critical point of decision at which you are able to see two major and divergent directions that your life could take. In one direction you can see fulfillment beckoning, the answer to your real needs and hopes. To step onto that path would mean bringing about what you really want.

In the other direction lie self-deception and illusion, the avoidance of real experience. To step onto that path would keep you embroiled in patterns of wishing without enacting. That would mean evading the fulfillment you aim for.

When thinking about this decisive point, we tend to say, 'Of course I shall commit to the path of fulfillment. After all, that is what I really want. Nothing else would make sense.'

What do you say? More importantly, what do you do?

Swimming anyone?

CHAPTER THIRTY-THREE

COMMITMENT TO SUCCESS

Commitment couples you to success. It is due to your commitment that you grow ever closer to your goal. Growth means changing and experiencing turmoil. Often it is only the strength of your commitment that determines whether you succumb to fear and confusion, or bear them steadily, in order to utilize their energy positively, while you proceed toward success.

A pilot commits himself to a well thought-out flight plan that will guide him toward his goal if he follows it faithfully. He does not abandon it when dark clouds appear, lest he become hopelessly lost, go in circles and crash after running out of fuel. It is precisely due to his commitment that he stays on his course, safely surviving momentary darkness, until he emerges and attains his goal. The pilot does not fear committing himself to a flight plan.

When you see yourself standing at the crossroads of life, you are challenged to respond and commit yourself to one direction or another. If you fear to make a commitment, remember this:

Not to make a commitment
is to commit yourself by default.

Life keeps moving. When we stand in fear and indecision, decisions are made for us. In passivity we are subject to irresponsibility, which connects us to self-deception and denial. Lack of trust in ourselves and insecurity are sure to follow. Thus it is clear to see that not making commitments creates indecisiveness leading to passivity, which, in turn, results in a life of hardship with the pain and sorrow we so much fear.

To save ourselves from such needless suffering, we sincerely determine to never again allow ourselves to become enslaved by lack of commitment. It makes no sense to spend precious life moments maintaining, reinforcing and even decorating the bridges that lead to nothing but disappointment and suffering.

You may wish to hike to a mountain top. Plans and preparations are made, but they become actualized only when you take that first step onto the path toward the top. You do not delay enjoying the mountain until you reach the top; you enjoy the path too, as it winds its way past obstacles and beautiful views.

To take the path leading to fulfillment
means to commit yourself
to what you really want.

It means to commit yourself to all you have learned, to the evidence of reality that you have gained through your experience, to real knowledge. Commitment to fulfillment means burning the bridges leading to self-distraction and limitation, and taking the decisive step that is but the first in a continuing series relating you to your goal. Then, what you have always wanted is recognized to be not some distant point, but the realm you are now experiencing.

*Commitment is
an indispensable ingredient of fulfillment.*

Commitment requires you to consciously choose among alternative answers to life's questions. Do you want to live in complete openness, or be partially hidden behind a protective wall? Do you face yourself or delude yourself? Do you live together or apart, interconnected or isolated? Commitment means aligning yourself with specific choices and assuming responsibility for those choices by integrating them into your existence, by living them. This is the great opportunity you have been working, wishing and waiting for throughout life.

*To commit yourself
is to bring together
what you want
with who you are
and what you do.*

THE POWER OF WILL

CHAPTER THIRTY-FOUR

THE TYRANNY OF NATURE
VS.
THE FREEDOM OF BEING HUMAN

The quest for peace is one of the historical themes of humanity as well as of our lives individually.

Deep within us there is a steady yearning for peace. We seek a state where harmony can flourish within ourselves as well as with our family, community and among nations. Nevertheless, we often suffer a distressing lack of peace.

We seem to find ourselves placed amidst nature's enormous churning forces, while somehow knowing of our own inherent power to live beyond her blindly driving processes. Human existence has been shaped not only by the onrush of nature's cataclysmic forces in our external environment, but—perhaps even more powerfully—by nature's processes within us. Yet we are aware of something about us that is transcendent.

Your life force,
the power that is your essence,
is to be experienced and expressed
in its fullness,
in its grand panorama
of infinite possibilities,
not limited to mere reactions to nature.

Every spring when I walk the trails through the chaparral, I see the hillsides highlighted with the beautiful tall flowers of the yucca plants. These spectacular creations rise from the decomposed remains of last year's beautiful plants, which had spent their final burst of energy producing the seed for the new. In plant life, the vital energy is completely absorbed by those repetitive cycles, thus limited to the physical realm.

Although in animals life is more varied and complex than in plants, the vital force is primarily absorbed in serving body and senses, thus still limited.

That is not enough for us. We cannot be at peace until our potential, our destiny, is fulfilled. Like lower life forms, we do feel the urge to take care of the basic physical needs. But as soon as the physical necessities have been taken care of, we become aware of further needs—deeper, subtler yearnings.

We require a life that includes, besides the physical necessities and sensual pleasures, the mental awareness of the life processes within and about us. We need the emotional satisfaction and security of being in harmony with the course of our existence. We long for the exhilaration of knowing the heights and depths of Being. We require the fulfillment of participating consciously in our evolution. That is a tall order. That is the life we are called upon to lead: the life of being human.

As human beings we have evolved to the state where we cannot indefinitely find refuge in slavery to circumstances.

Unlike the plant, we are not rooted to a spot, subject to the shifting modes of nature.

We have developed the capacity to participate knowingly in the course of our life, to respond on our own terms to changing conditions. In order to participate knowingly, we need to discriminate between the harmful and the beneficial, between that which hinders and that which empowers us to lead life according to our full—our truly human—potential.

Life never requires anything
without giving you the capability to fulfill it.

Not only are you capable of discrimination, you are also able to make choices. After assessing a situation, you choose how to respond, or you may even choose not to respond. You can walk toward the sun, or away from it, or you can stay where you happen to be. You have the freedom to choose active participation in life, or passive resistance to it.

To choose active participation in life
is to live up to your human potential;
to choose passive resistance to life
is to deny it.

It is in the active participation in your existence that you can find lasting success and final fulfillment.

CHAPTER THIRTY-FIVE

WILL: THE POWER TO BE HUMAN

My brother's name is Wilfried. "Wil" is the power by which we implement our choices; "Friede" means peace. This ancient name has always intrigued me. It places will and peace into an undeniable union, unequivocally affirming the intimate inter-connectedness between the power of will and the state of peace.

In spite of our demented attempts to present evidence to the contrary, there is in us an intrinsic drive to aspire to the state of harmonious integration of all the faculties within us individually and among us all collectively. That harmonious integration creates the state of peace.

No matter what rewards you gather
through your daily toil,
they are of no avail to you
if you cannot enjoy them
in the state of peace.

Through the evolutionary process we have evolved all the capacities by which we call ourselves human. It is specifically due to those capacities that we are able to rise above the conflicts which our existence in nature seems to present to us, and thereby realize a life that goes beyond those turmoils.

To transcend the limitations of nature is also the challenge of being human. It is due to your ability to discriminate and choose that you are able to respond to this challenge, to aspire to the potential of absolute fulfillment in Being.

Though discrimination and choice are wonderful powers, they, by themselves, are still not enough to provide you the fulfillment of your humanness. What good would your ability to discriminate and choose be, if you lacked the power to implement your choices? Life would be neither so cruel nor so illogical as to let such a condition prevail.

Will is the power
by which discrimination and choice
are brought to fruition.

It is will that differentiates us most of all from lower life forms. Will, wielded responsibly, with detachment and knowledge, qualifies us fully as human—thinking—beings.

Where do you go to acquire this will? Within. Nothing comes out of nothing. The energy of will is already within you. You just have to open yourself to it, to relate to it truthfully.

Will is the self-assertion
of the Power of Being.
It serves the infinite Power of Being
in self-expression and self-experience
and exists everywhere.
Will is universal
and belongs to the divine.

When we view will as belonging to separate individuals, to isolated ego identities, we taint our relationship to will with the same ignorance that so painfully distorts our faculties' relationship to ourselves. When we apply will in order to assert our ego—our false perception of ourselves—our relationship to will is inevitably distorted and causes pain. Only when we apply will as divine self-assertion do the consequences yield the real success and satisfaction we seek.

Will is to serve Self, not ego.
Thus, for your benefit,
you need to transform
your perception and assertion of will
from the egotistical
to the divine.

This is an important aspect on the path of becoming Expert In Life™ and Self-realized. In Self-realization you are true to the meaning of existence.

Existence is impartial in its justness. Just as life gives you the capability of fulfilling its requirements, so it requires of you the proper qualifications before allowing fulfillment.

As a human you are gifted with a potential for experience and expression—and consequent fulfillment—that is so subtle and far-ranging as to be limitless. What is fundamentally required of you is that you dedicate your potential fully and freely to the Being you really are. This dedication is to be confirmed by the commitment of the full force of your will.

You are called upon to be true to what you are:
human being
with discrimination, choice and will;
to live that,
express that,
and to enjoy every opportunity
to exercise those wonderful powers
with utmost skill.

Life challenges you to refuse being passively pushed around by circumstances, events, emotions, feelings or any other of the innumerable passing phenomena that tend to dictate your destiny. You are challenged to work through the maze of experiences by fully recognizing and committing your unique potential, and thereby claiming your human birthright: responsible participation in the course of your destiny.

This requires your total involvement in life and inspires you to pay your attention, apply your will and fine-tune your faculties to the utmost potential. Your finely attuned faculties will, in turn, empower you to experience life fully and express it fulfillingly.

Life makes you pay
and returns this payment
as your reward!

CHAPTER THIRTY-SIX

WILL: THE DIFFERENCE BETWEEN SUCCESS AND FAILURE

Life will not force its rewards upon you;
it will not cajole you or trick you
to accept its bounty.

A real love relationship between two individuals can only flourish by mutual consent. Life is a true lover to us— completely open and unfailingly honest. We are free to join with it on all levels, or to turn away from it.

To the degree
that you knowingly and willingly
merge with life,
you approach fulfillment;
to the degree
that you turn away from life,
you suffer.

243

The plant does not suffer due to the neglect of will, as we do, because it does not have will. We suffer when we do not implement the will we have. We suffer feelings of emptiness, fear, frustration and sorrow, even self-loathing, when our potential as human beings remains unfulfilled—when we are not yet living our full humanness.

> *There are as many ways*
> *of turning away from life*
> *as there are unfulfilled human beings.*

We all want fulfillment, and we have what we need to succeed. Often people ask me, "Why does it take so long? I know what I need to make my life fulfilling. I know what to do; I even know how to do it. Yet I don't. Over and over again I watch myself failing to do what I really want to do, and can do. Why?"

If we observe our ups and downs dispassionately, we can see how we divert ourselves from experiencing what we really want. Often, we set out to do something, even learn how to make it succeed, and then make ourselves fail. Why?

Many of us are not willing to commit the full force of will to our life, because that would mean being ultimately responsible.

Through the power of will you exercise your ability to have your faculties respond by working effectively for you. It is not enough to possess the faculties required for success; they must be willingly applied.

> *Will is the conscious power*
> *to actualize your intentions.*

You do not get what you want by merely wishing and wanting, theorizing and hypothesizing, nor by making faint passes at being real in your intentions—life is not some silly game. The deciding factor that makes reality of your intentions is will. By the proper application of will you convert your wishes and plans into actuality.

Sometimes you see people who can do exceptional things and be extraordinarily successful. They did not come into this life with any greater potential than the rest of us. Yet, they can do things that most people would never dare dream of. Why? Because they have developed their faculties and attuned them to a great degree of effectiveness by the power of their will. Nobody did it for them. It is the opportunity and privilege of every human being to develop their faculties, their abilities, talents and strengths to the fullest degree.

An instrument as powerful and fine as will deserves to be used with knowledge and skill. Do not think of will as brute force, but as a potent and refined impetus toward self-determination and Self-realization.

Purposefully train your body, your senses, nerves, reflexes and mind—even your thoughts and emotions—to relate subtly and skillfully to your will. Slough off the bondage of compulsions, for they only fill you with self-loathing and disgust.

Often people fail because they use their will against their own well-being. Will, like a sharp knife, can be used to effect great benefit, or to inflict terrible harm. To wield will in service to ego, or to waste it on passing fancies, dissipates our will power and brings great harm.

> *Do not devote your life energy*
> *to the pursuit of things*
> *that only disappoint you*
> *once you gain them.*

Free yourself from the entanglements you do not really want. You are human; you deserve so much more than that. Do not permit superficial glitter to lure you away from the experience of the beauty, the essence, the fulfillment that lies just behind it.

CHAPTER THIRTY-SEVEN

How To Succeed With Will

Your will is a great power that deserves to be cultivated by intelligent practice. Practice applying your will in a positive way. Decide that you will do something good for yourself that you have been wanting to do, but have neglected due to laziness, forgetfulness or insecurity. Choose a reasonable program that allows for success: try something small and build up from there.

Let us say you decide that for one week you will arise early enough to do some exercises before going to work. Think about it just long enough to be clear; then involve your will immediately, avoiding procrastination.

Remain calm and determined as you steadily apply your will in seeing this decision through to completion. Old patterns will tend to reassert themselves and try your will. You may have temptations of aimlessness, laziness, even fear. Do not mind, do not blame; just persevere. With faith in your strength and ability, you will succeed.

The next step is to recognize that accomplishment. This gives a great boost to your ability to persist. It is important that you acknowledge accomplishment instead of harping on failure.

The achievement of what you set out to do
is accomplished
by the persistent application of your will,
and is its own reward.

Let your success encourage you toward further positive assertions. Thus you use your will in purposefully building a more knowing and skilled relationship to the power of will. You exercise your ability to use will power by training yourself, progressing gradually from smaller to greater challenges.

It helps to remember that temptations will initially keep arising. So do not blame yourself for that—they, too, have their purpose. Too many people fail because they expect success after the first few attempts. They accuse themselves of failure merely because old habits refuse to die immediately.

Instead, see every temptation as an opportunity to react positively by asserting your will again. This increases the positive impressions already established, and makes will a more prominent factor in your life.

Recognize that giving in
to harmful temptations
destroys your advantageous relationship
to will.

You are gifted with the wonderful force of will and with the ability to use it positively. If you repeatedly fail, you slide into the habit of failure. This habit will soon become standard procedure, making success seem unfamiliar and even frightening. You then lose confidence in the power of will, and eventually forget its very existence. That is why it is so important to keep this fine faculty well honed.

A person of strong will removes such false ideas as, 'I can't,' 'Impossible' and 'Too difficult.' These are the expressions of the hesitant, of those who relate to themselves as weak, of those who wish and wait eternally.

Have the courage to be true to what you are and know. Choose to use your will for that responsibly, and live as a truly human being.

With sincere and consistent practice, definite results will be noticed by you as well as by others. You will feel in charge of your life, living and acting with self-respect and assurance. Work that you had previously regarded as a threatening imposition, you can now welcome with zest, and complete with skill and ease. Your mind will dwell in balance and will not be ruffled. Friends and family will enjoy your calming presence.

There is nothing surprising about all this. You benefit by your direct experience of freedom from the internal and external compulsions that had been the tyrants of your life. You know that such tyranny can enslave you only if you allow it. Once you assert your will sincerely, consistently and in accord with what your life is really about, nothing can prevail against you. So great is the power of will!

Will is the power by which your real Being
expresses itself in action.
By will you raise yourself
above the limited life experience
of plant and animal,
and avail yourself
of the full human potential.

Your limitless potential is realized when you act upon it—
when you live it—by the commitment of your free will.

The span of this life
is but a flash in eternity.
By the use of will,
you seize this rare moment
and turn it into endless opportunity
to experience great joy and lasting peace.

LIVING TRUE TO
THE BEING THAT YOU ARE

CHAPTER THIRTY-EIGHT

BEING THE SILENT OBSERVER

There is a wonderful state of being in which you can expand your perspective and free yourself from the dictatorship of negative, repressed, obsessive or otherwise dysfunctional thoughts, feelings and emotions. This state is called the Silent Observer. Only in this unhindered conscious state can you fully savor the experience of your real Being, irrespective of circumstances and conditions.

As the Silent Observer you are free
from attachment and consequent limitation.
You securely and calmly
accept what is,
including yourself.
Thus your energy is no longer occupied
with the constant sorting between
likes and dislikes,
desires and aversions,
even rights and wrongs.

You can learn to cultivate the state of Silent Observer to such strength and continuity that it becomes a powerfully balancing and illuminating aspect of your daily life activity and experience. Dwelling in this state you are free and fluid in your full power.

Usually we think of an observer as someone who stands outside of something and just watches. The Silent Observer is actively engaged in the experience of what is going on, but is not caught up in it. This is the important part. Once you are caught up in what is going on, you no longer have the full possibility of the moment—the wholeness of reality.

In order to deeply impress what you are about to learn here regarding the Silent Observer, you may choose to now cultivate the experiences suggested in this writing while you are reading about them.

To start, cause the muscles of your back to support your spine in a comfortably erect position. Feel the energy flowing up your back, free of impediment, steadily uplifting your torso. Tell your entire body to relax, from the crown of your head to the soles of your feet. Relax your whole body inside and out. Feel vibrant and light.

The easy movement of your abdominal muscles causes your breath to flow effortlessly. Inhale, and allow yourself to expand in the experience of the power and beauty of your Being. Be focused in the quietly balanced joy of recognizing the subtle pervasive power of the real Self that you are. Allow your breath to flow in easy rhythm. This rhythm affects body and mind; both assume a pose of effortless balance.

Remember: simply go along with these suggestions, step-by-step. You can do this regardless of any other activities. Just keep your mind alert and finely attuned. Relax.

You do not have to discuss this within yourself, nor need you question or dissect every little step; just trust in yourself and go along. Allow yourself the simple and clear experience of this moment of being. It will be deeply rejuvenating and revealing.

Promise yourself that you will easily maintain mental focus from moment to moment. Preserve a sense of effortless balance throughout.

Your mind can really rest now, reminded by the rhythm of your breath to be utterly calm. You can feel mind relax. It has gathered its divergent rays and rests in the resultant unity. There is no dissipation of mental energy.

When a feeling arises, simply allow it to be as it is. Neither hold it back, nor hold on to it. Just let it be. Do not judge it as right or wrong, desirable or undesirable. Just let it flow. Allow the feeling to be a momentary part of your experience of Being, and let it pass on. Whatever thoughts, feelings or emotions arise, allow them to flow in unhindered succession. You can simply let be the ways of experiencing that you are.

When mind is in service of the limited self—the false idea of your identity—it is scattered by the many operations of maintaining illusion and false conception. In this moment though, give your mind a rest from such burdensome activities; let it relax. This does not mean that your mind goes numb. On the contrary, as you remain in the attitude of the Silent Observer, your mind steadily expands to deeper and higher perception in dynamic stillness. The out-going activities are suspended. There is but clear, clean consciousness.

Now your mind is no longer enslaved by its involvement with false concepts. It is free to reflect your true identity, which is limitlessly conscious Being.

Experience yourself now as the Silent Observer: you are a calm witness who observes the operations of the mind, feelings and emotions, of the intellect, intuition, and even of the senses. The Silent Observer witnesses with total impartiality and absolute detachment.

Of course you are probably not used to being in such an unattached and impartial state. Relax. For now just let your mind be like a reflecting screen.

When your mind is enslaved by ego,
every thought is a distraction.
But when mind serves the true Self,
thoughts just appear on your mind
as if on a reflecting screen
and pass right on,
causing neither ripple nor wave
on the tranquil surface of mind.

Allow your mind to reflect purely to the Silent Observer. Again, cease the battles of deciding between good and bad; suspend judgment for now. You can accept the Being that you are, in reality, as it is. For this moment you have no obligations, no agenda. You can relax. You do not have to fragmentize or pull your mind in all directions; you can just rest from all that. In quiet balance simply observe with total impartiality and with absolute detachment. You are free from all rationalizations. Be at ease, be relaxed, quiet, calm.

In this beautifully balanced state of collectedness you are able to call upon the higher functions of your faculties: to participate without distortion in the totality of Being. As the Silent Observer you are aware of your thoughts, feelings and emotions, but you do not hold on to them. In your unattachment you are free to have them continuously serve you as the momentary colors and textures that enrich your experience of Being.

Imagine sitting with family and dear friends at holiday dinner. As the Silent Observer you savor the experience no matter what is going on. The events do not have to be interesting; experiencing your Being through these people is interesting enough. You can acknowledge and feel what you observe. Even if you observe a contrary feeling, you can allow it to pass by without being frustrated by it.

> *The Silent Observer does not reject*
> *any thought or feeling*
> *because the Silent Observer*
> *is centered in the Self,*
> *in the experience of Being,*
> *and has the freedom*
> *to allow thoughts and feelings to arise,*
> *to witness them*
> *and let them pass on.*

The whole experience of your silent observation is so precious and so enjoyable that your faculties are drawn to it—they want to be in it all the time. You will have the confidence of your power because you will experience yourself in terms of the universal power that you essentially are.

Unattached as the Silent Observer, you experience a continuous flow from moment to moment, event to event. It is only attachment to particular experience that halts the free flow of your full experience. You can have continuous experience of effortless Being through consistently maintaining the impartial Silent Observer state. So, simply—and simply is important here—with every breath, keep everything about you absorbed in the flow of comfortably and consciously experienced Being. You are that...

CHAPTER THIRTY-NINE

PRACTICING YOUR RESOLUTIONS

It is said that the road to hell is paved with good intentions. More accurately, it is paved not so much with good intentions, but with broken resolutions. Good intentions are not enough.

The road to fulfillment
is paved solidly with firm resolutions
reliably kept.

This takes practice. Firmly founded practice qualifies you for life expertise which, in turn, prepares you for a fulfilling life. In the ancient scriptures, The Yoga Sutras, the sage Patañjali states, "That practice, when continued constantly for a long time without break and with devotion, becomes firm in foundation."

Practicing to become Expert In Life™ and thus fulfilling your potential is not some outside thing you do now and then. Real practice is the sincere integration of all your daily involvements with your ultimate aim. This includes whatever you do to express and satisfy yourself physically, psychologically and mentally.

Everything in your life wants to be integrated with your constant practice toward life expertise: your activities at work; relationships with family and friends; and—not to forget— your life in your community, society, as well as your environment. Thus you relate to every moment, every circumstance and action as an opportunity to be continuously and consciously involved in leading your life according to your firm determination.

As we all have patterns of conditioning and habits that oppose such a clear life, we must not expect instant and all-inclusive success. That is where constant and extended practice comes in. Set your mind to it, take it seriously, and remind yourself as often as possible.

Gradually the patterns of positivity become natural and automatic to you, an integral aspect of your life. Then you need not aspire toward fulfillment in the future, but are aware of living it in the present moment.

You also need trust in yourself. You know that the distractions sometimes seem more appealing than what you have determined to do with your life. But you also know that their promise is false and leads only to disappointment. Trust in your knowledge.

The conduct of life
often comes down to a struggle
between your power to lead your life
and the factors within and around you
that want to seize your life.

You know that you have the power to prevail. Trust in that. There are times when it seems we are not making any progress in life. That is when trust in ourselves is extremely important. We trust that our growth continues steadily, though quietly, unsensationally, and that the flowering of it will unfold.

In this age of instant—but oh so superficial and passing—gratification, it is important for us to remember trust in ourselves. Self-trust allows us to be continuous in our life approach, empowering us to succeed ultimately—in the most profound and satisfying way.

The goal you aim at,
the fulfillment of your life's potential,
is the highest prize
of human achievement.

In the attainment of this goal, demands will be made on your physical, mental and spiritual resources. You learn to welcome that, for the demands challenge and strengthen you. They hone all your instruments to a fine point, empowering you to experience life so much more clearly.

It helps you to persevere
when you remember
that in aiming for something,
you cannot start at the end result;
the process is part of your pleasure.

While at times you will enjoy obvious progress, you must also be ready for slow and laborious growth. More often than not, the difference between failure and success is made by prevailing through the difficult times.

Keep in mind this promise, this guarantee:

> *If you proceed sincerely,*
> *with dedication,*
> *right knowledge*
> *and whole-hearted persistence,*
> *you will overcome,*
> *step-by-step,*
> *all hindrances, diversions and dissipations.*
> *You will transform these obstacles*
> *into steppingstones to success.*

Positive results will occur more easily and rapidly. They will reinforce each other in a chain reaction that cannot help but result in final fulfillment. You will be filled and inspired with a sense of awe and exhilaration as you become conscious of the enormous wealth and potential within you.

CHAPTER FORTY

FULFILLMENT IN
THE NEW MILLENNIUM

As we consider the new millennium, we collectively look at the past as well as the present and future with self-assessment and fresh new hope growing out of a deep knowledge of great potential resting within.

There is in us a desire for the newness that is part of a beginning. We like starting afresh with a clean slate, uncluttered by the failures suffered in the past and the aspirations not fulfilled.

When contemplating the great changes awaiting us in the new millennium, it behooves us to consider that, most likely, we are already engaged in a quiet and subtle, yet deep-reaching change process. In nature, for example, winter is a season of dormant potential. Our prospects may seem quite bleak when much of the land is covered by snow, with hostile winds and freezing temperatures causing considerable discomfort.

The barren bleakness of winter is only a passing appearance however, for underneath the frozen blanket of snow, life is busily doing its subtle work, preparing to spring forth and flower in beautiful, new expressions as soon as the snow melts. And so it is with us.

Deep in our core is the pervasive stirring of vitality wanting to express itself in energetic growth. We are called to awaken, stretch our limbs and open our eyes to our real Self, to the wholeness of our Being. No matter how bleak life may at times seem, our vital force is not to be denied. This is true of us individually as well as collectively.

With the change of millennia we are inspired to respond with determination to the deep stirrings within. We can make a firm resolution toward positivity and self-direction, to live in honesty and clarity, true to the Being we really are. We feel uplifted by the anticipation of the joy and satisfaction we are sure to derive. If the mere anticipation can give us such positive results, how much greater the benefits when we actually carry out our resolution.

But all too often most of us run into trouble when it comes to fulfilling what we set out to do. We make strong positive resolutions, we make them sincerely and even feel good about them, and somehow fail to follow through.

What happens? We are busy, we forget. The clear energy with which we made our resolutions is diverted again by the distractive onslaught of the innumerable details and demands of day-to-day life.

Even on national or societal levels our response to our resolutions is often not very different. Distracted by shortsightedness, selfishness and internal conflicts, whole nations can lose sight of the positive future they had charted for themselves, only to feel bogged down in the negativity of the moment.

Here we have to remember, though, that we are in charge of this life as well as the future of humanity. It makes no sense to allow the obstacles to take over and prevent us from doing what we have determined we really want to do.

There is also the important matter of integrity.

> *If we respect ourselves enough*
> *to be true to our determinations,*
> *we will respect others sufficiently*
> *to keep our promises to them.*

The foundation of self-respect will build trust and cooperation leading to unity among nations.

We will benefit profoundly, individually and as humanity, when we consistently treat our resolutions for a better life—our promises to ourselves—with self-respect. We must not allow our determinations to be subsumed by a busy life. Our integrity demands it.

Pursuing an ultimately successful life, one that is truly ours and is truly fulfilling, need not be viewed as a threat or a burden, nor is it to be relegated to the realms of hobbies or fantasies. We only dismiss ourselves and our potential when we are too distracted or confused to be in touch with our internal voice, the Inner Knower who has never led us astray.

> *Our situation is not a hopeless one.*
> *The suffering we undergo,*
> *as well as the joy we experience,*
> *has as its real purpose*
> *to alert and guide us*
> *toward deeper understanding of ourselves,*
> *and thereby*
> *to the fulfillment of our potential.*

We can learn to be guided by the challenges and opportunities of the new millennium and therefore to benefit from them.

Through growing in our understanding of what we really are and have, and following through on our determination, we learn to create more functional responses to our world, our lives and ourselves. This will accelerate our growth into full power and joy as vibrantly alive and functional individuals, and as harmonious societies fundamentally united. Thus empowered, we can consciously direct ourselves as one humanity onto the quantum steps of evolution of which we are so capable.

This is my wish for us all: that we succeed in fulfilling what we really want and thus assure a successful and deeply satisfying life, as well as a new millennium that sees the advancement of humanity toward the realization of our full potential in Being.

May the generations that succeed us
look back as we do now
and appreciate the wise choices we make
for the new millennium.
May our choices and resolve
empower our offspring
to lead a positive life toward the fulfillment
of their and their children's potential.
May we learn from the past
and empower our future.

GLOSSARY OF TERMS

awareness: conscious experience.

being: existing; manifesting Being; a manifestation of Being.

Being: the essential, all-pervasive, enduring, unifying and united power by which everything is; the irreducible identity of all life forms.

Beingness: term used to emphasize Being, the identity, over being, the act.

bliss: transcendent joy integral to the clear, undistracted and continuous experience of Being.

body: the physical/material apparatus of a being.

cause and effect: the law of nature relating all actions inexorably with their consequences.

center: a focal point in meditation, the area of your heart, which is limitless, free of boundaries; where you experience the awareness of Being, the light of consciousness.

circumstances and conditions: the ephemeral, the impermanent; the opposite of essence.

commitment: aligning yourself with a specific choice and assuming responsibility for that choice by integrating it into your existence, by living it.

concentration: the gathering of your energies (mental, emotional, intellectual, intuitional, physical and sensual) and fixing them at will upon a chosen point.

conditioning: patterns of reaction and behavior established through repetition.

conscious experience: being aware of Self purely, or in relation with objects and events (physical, sensual, emotional, mental, intellectual or intuitional).

consciousness: the awareness/experience of Being.

core: your center of Being.

creative force: Being expressing Self.

crisis: the effect caused by not responding to the reality of Being.

crossroads: a critical point of decision regarding two major and divergent directions your life could take—fulfillment in reality or suffering in self-deception.

darkness: the absence of the light of self-awareness.

death: when a current manifestation of Being ends and changes into another state of being.

denial: refusal to acknowledge reality.

depression: a dysfunctional state resulting from the repression of feeling.

destiny: the course of life molded by what you come into this life with and the conditioning and habits established in this life, as well as your determined actions.

detachment: not involving yourself in particulars at the expense of your involvement in the infinite wholeness.

disease: the breakdown of the integration of the various aspects of your Being; imbalance.

dysfunction: self-opposing behaviors resulting from being out of touch with your real Self.

ego: the false perception of identity as an isolated body-mind-emotions-feelings-intellect-intuition construct.

emotion: an expressive state; a subtle, internal response to an experience.

equanimity: balance; evenness of mind.

essence: that which makes you what you are; the absolute, irreducible substance of you; that which upholds everything about you; your unchanging identity; that without which you could not be.

evolution: growth toward integration with the whole; continuous process of development toward a state free of limitation; the process by which the manifestations of Being grow toward recognition of themselves as the one limitless Being they really are.

existence: that which is being.

experience: the undergoing of things generally, be they internal events—such as sensations, emotions, feelings, thoughts or intuitions—or external events; the process of encountering Being through its manifestations; the totality of your perceived and remembered encounters with Being.

experience of Being: the process of consciously encountering Being; being conscious.

Expert In Life™: a fundamental concept based on the recognition that our expertise in consciously utilizing our faculties toward the fulfillment of our life's meaning and the realization of our potential is of cardinal importance.

faculties: your instruments for experiencing and expressing Being, including body, senses, mind, emotions, feelings, intellect and intuition.

feeling: a perceptive state; a subtle, internal experience in relation to inner or outer conditions.

focus: to draw your attentiveness together.

frustration: the painful feeling experienced as a result of dwelling in a state contrary to who you really are and what you really want.

fulfillment: the state resulting from the experience of your infinite interconnectedness in which you realize that you are all and have all; the cessation of need.

guide: teacher on the spiritual path.

health: fully balanced system of forces.

identity: the irreducible and permanent factor without which you could not be; who you are essentially.

Inner Knower: the serene honest voice within that guides you with its utterly reliable truth.

integrity: being true to reality, to who you are and to your knowledge and your determination.

intellect: the power of knowing that includes the ability to extrapolate and reason.

interconnectedness: unrestricted union.

intuition: your subtle ability of immediate cognition without evident rational thought or sensory experience.

knowledge: to have cognition of something as the result of direct experience.

learning: the life process of acknowledging and integrating experience of reality.

love: unconditional acceptance; the harmonious realization of fundamental essence shared.

manifestation: the expression of Being.

mantra: distilled positive energy which is a pure aspect of essential reality, expressed in the form of a word or word phrase, that can be used to align all your faculties in the same positive vibratory pattern.

mantra practice: a complex physiological-psychological-spiritual discipline which purifies, refines and empowers your faculties for the experience of Being.

meditation: the unalloyed experience of Being, including the knowledge of what Being is, with clarity and continuity, without distraction and at will.

mind: the faculty that gathers input from the other faculties and coordinates and reflects it for your experience.

negative: that which conceals, obscures or distorts the experience of real Being; that which is ultimately disadvantageous.

objects: phenomena caused by the coming and going of atoms creating the appearance of material of shape and weight.

path: the way to fulfillment in reality.

phenomena: momentary events; the passing.

positive: that which reveals and contributes to the experience of real Being; that which is ultimately advantageous.

potential [human]: the full capability of all our faculties; living in the full continuous consciousness of infinite Being.

Power of Being: the power or energy that gives everything the ability to be; the substance of all that is.

practical: actually works toward accomplishing the goal.

practice: the repeated, intelligent use of a faculty by will.

procrastination: the act of indefinitely delaying the fulfillment of your intentions.

rationalization: lying to yourself.

reality: that which is, independent of circumstance, condition, time and space; the underlying absolute.

realize: make real by living it.

resistance: that which opposes change; that which keeps you from realizing true Self.

responsibility: the ability to respond.

right action: actions related expertly to who you really are.

seer: one who experiences and lives the transcendent and ultimate reality.

self: limited ego concept.

Self: your unchanging identity; that which you are essentially; the irreducible substance without which you could not be.

self-discipline: the study of the Self; actions chosen to express Self, sometimes in opposition to prevailing tendencies.

self-empowered: acting in the experience and expression of real Self.

Self-realization: knowledge of Self that is actualized by living, experiencing and expressing it; being congruent with knowledge of Self and thus freed from identification with the limiting ego construct.

senses: the perceptive capabilities by which you relate to the material realm: taste, smell, hearing, sight and touch.

Silent Observer: unattached witness to all events, external and internal.

soul: essence, spirit.

spirit: the essence; the true intent or meaning of something.

spiritual life: to live in loyalty and devotion to your spirit.

stress: the continuous experience of unrelieved tension caused by the breakdown of the harmonious balance of the faculties resulting from responding to situations or circumstances in the unawareness of Being.

Stress Release Response™: a set of seven steps by which you can dependably free yourself from stress and its harmful effects—at a few moments' notice and at will.

student: limitless Being in the guise of separateness who is being guided by limitless Being in interconnectedness who helps the seemingly disconnected recognize interconnectedness.

suffering: the result of ignorance regarding, or disregard of your true Self.

teacher: infinite Being manifesting in the self-awareness of all-pervasive interconnectedness guiding those manifestations who are in the illusion of separateness, toward the realization of their interconnectedness.

transcendent: beyond the limits and qualifications of time and space.

transformation: permanent change.

truth: that which unequivocally is.

unattachment: see *detachment.*

universal: all-inclusive; without limit or exception.

will: the power by which you implement your choices.

wisdom: knowledge gained by experience of reality continuously applied to your behaviors and actions.

yoga: the cessation of the modifications of the mind; the experience of the unitive state; the multi-faceted discipline and approach of realizing the unitive state.

PHOTOGRAPH CAPTIONS
All Photographs By Erhard Vogel

Page xxi
Winter Birches
New York state

Page 37
Hong Kong Harbor

Page xiii
Oil lamp

Page 41
Mogul tower
Old Delhi, India

Page 1
Mineral deposits
Turkey

Page 47
St. John, Cathedral of
Chartres
France

Page 3
Marble stairs
Assisi, Italy

Page 53
Tree alley
Hamburg, Germany

Page 15
Village women at
lake
Udaipur, India

Page 55
Coppersmith
Teheran, Iran

Page 17
Young shopkeeper
Kabul, Afghanistan

Page 63
Mosque
Iran

Page 23
Happy beggar
Kabul, Afghanistan

Page 69
Street scene
New York City

Page 27
Basket weaver & son
Udaipur, India

Page 75
Frozen lake
Colorado

Page 33
Village elder
Udaipur, India

Page 85
Greek ruin
Turkey

Page 91
Flute player
Kabul, Afghanistan

Page 99
Young shopkeepers
Kabul, Afghanistan

Page 109
Red Fort Palace
Old Delhi, India

Page 111
Mosque ceiling
Isfahan, Iran

Page 119
Mosque detail
Isfahan, Iran

Page 125
Banyan tree roots
Himalayas

Page 127
Young shopkeeper
Kabul, Afghanistan

Page 135
Memorial to a hero
Khyber Pass,
Afghanistan

Page 141
Zebra

Page 145
Saints, Cathedral of
Chartres
France

Page 151
Prayer at mosque
Isfahan, Iran

Page 153
Park
Hamburg, Germany

Page 159
Young shopkeeper
Kabul, Afghanistan

Page 163
Village women
mourning
Udaipur, India

Page 169
View of Ganges
from cave
Himalayas, India

Page 175
View from cave
Himalayas, India

Page 179
Ancient mosque
Iran

Page 181
Mosques & harbor
Istanbul, Turkey

Page 189
Ganges bank at
Varanasi
India

Page 195
Greek marble cause-
way
Turkey

Page 201
Taj Mahal
Agra, India

Page 203
Child
China

Page 207
Mogul gateway ruin
Old Delhi, India

Page 215
Stained glass window
Cathedral of
Chartres
France

Page 223
Gospel singers
New York City

Page 227
Mosque
Iran

Page 231
Cedar of Lebanon

Page 233
Greek amphitheatre
Turkey

Page 237
Canal
Venice, Italy

Page 243
Bell tower
Italy

Page 247
Ancient bazaar
Iran

Page 253
Sleeping Buddha
Ajanta, India

Page 255
Service entrance
Taj Mahal
Agra, India

Page 261
Sikh Golden Temple
Amritsar, India

Page 267
Winter Birches
detail

INDEX

For more than 30 years, Dr. Erhard Vogel has been guiding people to realize their true Being and contribute to the improvement of the human condition. He is recognized around the world as a Master Teacher of Self-realization.

"Self-realization," he writes, "is what all life strives for. It is making real our deepest longings and highest aspirations by living, experiencing and expressing our real identity, and thereby fulfilling our life potential." Dr. Vogel has based a lifetime of service on the conviction that Self-realization is the birthright of every human being.

Born in war-torn Germany in 1939, Erhard spent his childhood learning to survive the destruction around him. Facing death at a young age during the bombardments, he developed the determined focus to overcome his own fear and achieve clear experience of the meaning and purpose of life. Thus began his quest to develop the ways to live in lasting fulfillment.

Erhard emigrated to the United States at age 14 and worked to put himself through school. He graduated from the Pratt Institute of Design in New York, and as an architect rose to a respected position in a world-renowned design firm. At age 31, he set aside a brilliant career in architecture to devote himself to the service of humanity.

For four years Erhard traveled the globe on foot. He lived in the Arab nations, Iran, Afghanistan, India and Nepal, thoroughly researching the ways in which people of different cultures seek fulfillment. He saw the underlying need in everyone to fulfill their potential.

Erhard returned to the West with his teachings to address the problems and aspirations of our contemporary society. Following a lecture tour spanning the University system of the United States, as well as parts of Europe and Canada, Erhard came to San Diego, California, where in 1974 he founded the Nataraja Yoga Ashram, a not-for-profit social service organization.

Dr. Vogel's teachings are a unique combination of time-tested wisdom and pragmatic methods. His fundamental, systematic approach is based upon sound psychological, physiological and spiritual principles that make meditation and Self-realization practical and attainable. He teaches not from books nor from other people's ideas, but out of his own profound life experience.

Since 1969, Dr. Vogel has taught tens of thousands of students throughout the world. In addition to personally teaching the principal classes at the Nataraja Yoga Ashram, he lectures, conducts workshops and teacher training courses, writes books and records CDs. Dr. Vogel has the unique privilege of teaching regularly among the sages of the Himalayas. He holds a Ph.D. in Clinical Psychology. His most recent publication, *Journey Into Your Center*, adds another important work to an already impressive list of publications. The book was honored by being selected as one of three finalists for the 2001 Independent Publishers' Best Book of the Year Award.

The Nataraja Yoga Ashram is an organization for Self-realization. Established in 1974 in San Diego, California, as a not-for-profit social service organization, the Nataraja Yoga Ashram provides in-depth experiential teachings of expert ways to lead a fulfilling and successful life that is realistically directed toward the attainment of Self-realization in this lifetime.

Through an array of on-site programs and services, as well as world-wide correspondence courses, the Nataraja Yoga Ashram is dedicated to promoting the physiological, psychological and spiritual welfare of the human being.

The Expert In Life™ program was developed by Dr. Vogel over a lifetime of direct experience to provide the means by which to live in the state of Self-realization: fully self-aware and self-accepting, free from limitation, in deep inner peace and quietly balanced joy.

The Expert In Life program is a graduated group process centered around pro-active life application practices and strengthened by a shared commitment to success. It is the objective of the Expert In Life program to empower students to become expert at understanding, fine-tuning and strengthening their faculties so that they can harmoniously integrate and skillfully apply them toward real fulfillment.

ORDER FORM

Fax: (619) 443-4164
Phone: (619) 443-4164
Web: www.evogel.net
Mail: Nataraja Publications
          10171 Hawley Road
          San Diego, CA 92021

Nataraja Publications

Please send the following BOOKS, CDs and/or TAPES:

_____

_____

_____

_____

Name   _____

Address   _____

City/State/Zip   _____

Phone   _____

email   _____

Payment: Check Number: _____

      Visa / Mastercard: _____

          Card Number   _____

          Name on Card   _____

          Exp. date   _____

          (Please provide billing address if different from above.)

Sales tax: Please add 7.75% for products shipped to California addresses.

Shipping::   US: $4.95 for the first book and $2.00 for each additional
                  $3.95 for the first CD or tape and $1 for each additional
          Intl: $10.00 for first book and $5.00 for each additional
                  $7.00 for the first CD or tape and $2 for each additional

Visit us on the web
w w w . e v o g e l . n e t